SPIRITUAL WISDOM

SPIRITUAL WISDOM

Practical spirituality for people today

Claire Montanaro

PIATKUS

PIATKUS

First published in Great Britain in 2008 by Piatkus Books Ltd

Copyright © 2008 by Claire Montanaro

Reprinted 2008 (twice)

The moral right of the author has been asserted

A CIP catalogue record for this book
is available from the British Library

ISBN 978-0-7499-2874-2

Typeset in Stone Serif by M Rules
Printed and bound in Great Britain by
CPI Antony Rowe, Chippenham, Wilts

Piatkus Books
An imprint of
Little, Brown Book Group
100 Victoria Embankment
London EC4Y 0DY

An Hachette Livre UK Company
www.hachettelivre.co.uk

www.piatkus.co.uk

To Jim, who has kept me company
and been my loving guardian and protector for ever.

Contents

Acnowledgements

I give my loving thanks and appreciation to my friends in this world and beyond for their support and understanding of my spiritual journey and their unfailing belief in me.

I give my thanks to the Lucis Trust for permission to quote from the Alice Bailey material. Much of my knowledge of the subjects covered in this book derives from or was stimulated by her writings in particular, and I am grateful to be able to use them as one of a number of foundation stones for my work. I give thanks also to Michael D. Robbins, author of *Tapestry of the Gods* for permission to quote from his material in the chapter on the Seven Rays.

Every effort has been made to give attribution to these and other authors who have played their part in the writing of *Spiritual Wisdom*, and I include a bibliography of those works that have contributed to the information put forward or which may assist or expand your understandings of the subjects covered. I do not endorse, necessarily, all the ideas or arguments of the authors and books listed.

I am grateful also to Helen Stanton and Gill Bailey of Piatkus Books for having faith in the concept of *Spiritual Wisdom*, and for their encouragement during the time of its conception, development and birth, and to Anne Jones, gifted healer, writer and dear friend for her part in its creation.

Introduction

Spiritual Wisdom is a book that in so many ways should not have been written. Until I was heading comfortably towards middle age I had no interest in spirituality at all and my ignorance about such matters was almost total. My life was the epitome of conventionality – born into a middle-class military family, the eldest of six children, grammar school, university and then joining the army myself and serving around the world for 16 years. There was marriage and then a civilian career as a political lobbyist for a leading British bank, and it was during this time that I received my spiritual wake-up call.

Until then my focus had been on doing my job as best I could, on being what was expected of me socially and societally (the perfect hostess, the dutiful daughter, a high achiever, immaculate clothes and make-up, the latest 'must-have' . . .) with the result that I was, I realise now, from my early childhood always striving to be someone other people wanted me to be rather than myself. People saw what appeared to be an enviable life of success and recognition, international travel, a good income and a busy social life, but in fact I was so stressed I developed a serious back problem, and had no sense of fun or joy, only responsibility. I was not very happy in my life, particularly since the burden of trying to be someone I was not led to massive self-judgement, guilt and fear of failure.

Then my world was turned upside down overnight and was never to be the same again.

It was on 11 January 1995 that it happened. My route home from my job in the City was a train ride to Chorleywood and then a short walk down a steep uneven path which led from the station to the village where I lived. Normally the path was well lit by several street lights, but that night every light was out and it was in complete darkness. I was the first commuter to leave the station: unable to see anything, I moved ahead gingerly but despite my care I caught my heel in a deep rut and fell forward.

As I went down I felt myself being picked up and then, three times, my head was smashed on the ground. I have been told by a witness that, from behind, it looked as if my body bounced down the hill like a toy. I was knocked out, unsurprisingly, and came round to find a group of concerned fellow-travellers surrounding me, one of whom helped me home where my husband was waiting for me. I was in a bad state — sore, faint and shaken with my face swelling already and covered in blood, so he helped me clean myself up and put me to bed.

I was concussed and in shock and went into a deep sleep immediately. It was about three hours later that I was roused from my sleep as if I had been tapped on the shoulder. I opened my eyes and saw standing at the bottom of my bed the figure of a man dressed in robes with shoulder-length wavy hair. He was as tall as the height of the room and broad commensurately, and I could see him clearly. It was a most beautiful face, with remarkable, unforgettable eyes which looked straight into mine with great intensity and seriousness. I gazed back. I felt no fear. I was calm but puzzled, wondering who this was and if it were a dead relative who was visiting me. In my mind I went through all the possibilities but was unable to match him to anyone I had known.

He and I continued to look at each other for some time until eventually I was released and went back to sleep. I know now it was the Christ, the World Teacher, who came to me.

The next day I discussed what had happened with my husband, who had slept through the experience much to his chagrin, and neither of us could explain it. As my face and body recovered from the fall everything seemed to return to normal, except that I was left with a vague sense of longing and dissatisfaction with my life and the desire to do something to help in the world – though without knowing what or how.

To cut a long story short, soon after that I met someone locally who introduced me to the concept of chakras and I was away. My spiritual journey, begun many lifetimes before, had resumed and my life was changed for ever. I was no longer interested in being the image of the dedicated professional businesswoman I had cultivated for so long, but was focused on helping others to achieve peace of mind, heart and soul through spiritual understanding where I could.

The path of learning and remembering was rapid and wonderful to me, and I am filled with gratitude for my wake-up call and the opportunities which came from it. It was as if a veil had been lifted and I found as I read and studied ancient texts and modern spiritual theories that I knew already, innately, much of what I was given and could discern what, for me, was accurate or not so accurate. The acceptance and application of these truths into my life helped me see the totality of who I am as part of the cosmic whole, and it transformed and enriched my existence.

A psychic unfolding occurred also and I found I had abilities as a medium, clairvoyant and channel that, before, I would not have believed was possible. Clients came to me more and more for help and guidance and I began to run spiritual development classes for people, in groups and also through the Internet, to help them expand their level of consciousness and to teach them the core spiritual truths. Requests for me to speak on these matters publicly came to me and my work expanded to become international.

I found, as I taught the spiritual wisdoms, that many people wanted to know where they could learn more about this subject, and while I could point them to this book or that book, I knew of no publication that drew the information together comprehensively and in a format that was easily understandable and that was practical for today's world. Thus was *Spiritual Wisdom* born.

While my wake-up call was dramatic, it does not mean that in order to be reminded of *your* spirituality you must have the same sort of experience as I did. It may be that it happened that way for me because I was particularly stubborn or reluctant to see what was in front of me! It is different for everybody and some people are drawn onto their path as a child, some when they are in their seventies, some not for a lifetime. Each person's soul path is unique to them and how they tread their journey will differ, but every one is equally valid and important.

The spiritual truths apply to all souls and every reader who is drawn to my book can benefit from it if they wish to at whatever degree they choose. It can be *your* wake-up call, an educational tool or something to dip in and out of when you feel like it – you will know how and how far it can serve you. If you resonate strongly with all or part of the book it is likely to indicate that an ancient memory of the wisdoms has been touched and brought back to the forefront of your consciousness to help you in this lifetime. If something I have written doesn't make sense or you disagree with it, you can put it to one side and move on.

Some of the information that I am passing on to you is, as far as I know it, new in the sense that I have not seen it given elsewhere. Other wisdoms that I write about here you may have heard or read in other places, but my interpretation may be rather different and it is for you to decide what you choose to take as accurate. Nothing that I say about spiritual truths, development or practice is compulsory and there is no right or wrong – there is only freedom of choice to follow what feels right to you.

For me, as I resumed my spiritual journey once again, my greatest teacher was Alice Bailey who wrote a series of twenty-four 'Blue Books' in the first half of the twentieth century, covering many of the key spiritual truths. Another writer who influenced me was Helena Blavatski, who lived in the nineteenth century. As a result of the eras in which they lived their style of writing is, to many people now, complex and their concepts difficult to grasp, so they are not widely read or indeed known these days, except in esoteric circles. I have no doubt of the enduring truths of which they wrote, and I have tried to present them, where it is appropriate, in a way that is accessible and understandable for readers of this book.

Most seekers of spiritual truth accept that God – whatever that is – exists and is the foundation stone for that truth. It is my belief also, and that premise is the life blood of this book. So, the word 'God' will appear frequently on these pages, but that word has many perfectly valid alternatives. I know that some of you are uncomfortable with a word that, for you, may denote authority, masculinity, disempowerment, punishment, wrath or which conflicts with your religious beliefs. Many of the negative associations come from the Old Testament, religious teaching, even past life memory, and I have encountered many clients and students who, while being very keen to progress their spiritual path, could not accept the term 'God' because of their memories of lifetime after lifetime of being punished in the name of God through persecution, perhaps, or harsh monastic life.

For now, as you read my book, I invite you to see God, quite simply, as Love, the Source of All. God can be known also as Light, as Spirit, as the First Creator, the Divine Masculine and Feminine, Life, the Totality, or even the Universal Mind. All of these terms are reasonable and indeed I believe that they are all part of the Being that I call God. So, when you see me use the word 'God' please understand what I am meaning by it – but it is, of course, your choice as to how you yourself view the concept and how far you accept and believe my ideas about God's place in your soul journey.

Incidentally, for ease of reference and brevity I may refer to God as 'He'. Please know that when I do so I am not being sexist and that the use of the word implies the feminine as much as the masculine. This applies to the use of 'he' as meaning men and women in other contexts also.

This is what the book is about:

- *Spiritual Wisdom* shows that spirituality is no longer just for mystics but is a practical tool based on common sense to bring about positive change in your life with results that are measurable.

- It describes what being spiritual means and how simple and accessible it is in reality.

- It explores in detail the many different aspects of karma and how, profoundly, it influences your human experience and your soul's journey.

- It looks at reincarnation, life and death. I have a strong belief in the concept of reincarnation, and open-mindedness to, at least, if not acceptance of, the idea will be helpful to maximise the value of the book for you. The meticulous planning and procedures for being born and reborn are described, and also the purpose behind your every lifetime. There is explanation about what happens during the dying process, how to manage it and what happens afterwards. Death is demystified, to be seen as a celebration and very special, not as an event to be feared.

- It explains the cohesion between spirit, soul and personality as part of the journey of the soul, and shows how you can enhance these connections.

- It enables you to track the journey of your soul from its inception, explaining the tests and challenges that are presented to you along the way and how to deal with them.

- It describes the influences that shape your world and affect you most profoundly, such as the energetic Rays; the great cycles of time, of Light and Dark and of materialism and altruism; and describes also your non-physical spiritual helpers – all influences you may not know exist or be aware of. One of the key reasons I wrote this book is to help you understand and use these forces to maximise your potential as a spiritual being and in your everyday life.

- It considers the ancient Spiritual Laws, such as the Law of Attraction (whereby you draw to yourself what you are focused upon through the power of your thoughts) and shows how applying the Laws to your life can bring you to a state of balance and harmony.

- Practical advice and exercises are included in every section if you wish to explore your spirituality further and expand your level of consciousness.

Writing this book has been a labour of love. I am the messenger. I wish you joy with it and a heartfelt hope that the knowledge within stirs your soul as it did, and does still, for me.

A NOTE ABOUT MEDITATION

You will find several references to meditation in the course of this book, also a number of meditation-based exercises, and so it may be helpful at this stage for me to give you some guidance about the subject. Now, meditation is not a mandatory part of being spiritual! However, it is an excellent way to encourage a sense of peace and calm within yourself, as well as helping you to develop your relationship with your spiritual helpers and the spiritual realms generally.

There are many different ways to meditate and you will find through practice the one that suits you best. A simple but effective way is to put aside some time, on a daily basis if you can, to sit quietly with an empty mind, just 'being'. It quietens the mind wonderfully and can bring about a profound sense of spiritual connection. I recommend it highly, particularly for those who are starting out on their active spiritual path.

Other people meditate using music or guided visualisation, chanting or toning, holding crystals or a sacred object, even through walking in nature. Many books are available to guide you through the alternative methods of meditating if you are interested in exploring the options. The techniques I outline here are ones that I have found useful for me personally and which many of my students have also found to bring about great benefits for them.

If you decide to try them for yourself, please read through the instructions thoroughly before you begin and follow them carefully. If you feel any strain or discomfort, please pause, gently, or cease your meditation altogether, ensuring you are back in your everyday reality completely before resuming your day. I will explain how you do this later in this chapter.

A word about the chakras

Because the chakras are an important element in your meditation practice, as well as for your spiritual development and understanding, I would like to say something here about the chakra system. You will find more information about them throughout the rest of the book.

A chakra is an energy point situated in a specific part of the body. The word itself is Sanskrit (the ancient Indian language) for spinning wheel. Chakras are part of very ancient Eastern spiritual traditions going back to 6000 BC or before, and they have been associated with yogic philosophy and practice in particular since the seventh century. Their importance is widely recognised and accepted in the West now.

As the chakras are an important element in your meditations, as well as for your spiritual development and understanding, I would like to say something at this point in the book about the chakra system. The information that I am giving you about them – number, location, colour and so on – is what is generally accepted as accurate, though you may find certain schools of thought have different ideas depending on their spiritual beliefs and traditions.

There are seven principal chakras, or energy centres, and for you as a human they are related to the spine and the endocrine glands. It is not just people who have a chakra system, you see. Earth has one, each country has one, each mountain or river has one, all animals have one too. The chakra points of a geographical area can be very powerful both spiritually and energetically, and ley lines (lines of strong spiritual energy on which sacred sites are often found) are often associated with them.

Chakras are connectors to the soul and spirit and keep you in balance spiritually, mentally, emotionally and physically. If a chakra is blocked or is not functioning properly, then the corresponding part of your life will be affected. When all your chakras are 'spinning' clearly and freely you will be living in perfect health at all levels.

The seven chakras are:

- First: **the base or root chakra** which is situated at the very bottom of the spine. Its colour is red and it grounds you in the physical world.

- Second: **the sacral chakra** is just above the pubic area. It is orange and concerns creativity and reproduction.

- Third: **the solar plexus chakra** is above the navel and is known as the seat of the emotions. It is yellow.

- Fourth: **the heart chakra** is, as you might expect, over the heart area, and it is pink or green. It deals with love and compassion, both for yourself and for giving out to others.

- Fifth: **the throat chakra** is over the throat. It is blue and deals with the different aspects of communication.

- Sixth: **the 'third eye' chakra** is between the eyebrows and is indigo in colour. This chakra concerns psychic abilities – literally using a psychic 'eye' to see beyond the world of matter.

- Seventh: **the crown chakra** is violet and is situated on the top of the head. It concerns your spirituality and your connection to God.

If you are in meditation and wish to heighten your spiritual awareness and connections it helps to focus on each chakra and to see or sense it opening up like a flower unfurling its petals, or as a spiral spinning faster and faster. It is important to remember to close down the chakras when you have finished your spiritual work by 'seeing' the flower petals return to being a bud, or the spiral ceasing to spin, or even a shutter or curtain coming down over each one. To be out and about in a busy world with your chakras open completely will make you more sensitive and vulnerable to any negative energies you may encounter.

Now, after that little digression, back to meditation . . .

General guidelines on meditating

If you can, do your meditation at the same time every day, preferably in the morning soon after you have got up. Your mind should be awake but not distracted by work, family or phone calls and so choose a time when you will not be disturbed. If the morning is impossible, then do it at whichever time of day is most suitable for you. For some people the only way is to snatch some time at lunchtime at their desk at work. If that is so, it is not ideal but much better than not doing it at all.

Similarly, if at all possible, try to sit in a place that is set aside just for your meditation so that it truly becomes your sacred space. If you don't have much room, it doesn't matter if it is a chair in the corner of your bedroom. Try to avoid using the place where you peel the potatoes or where people are in and out all the time, like a hallway! It is good if *your* energies can fill that space and no one else's.

When you have, hopefully, found your sacred space you might wish to place some special objects there to remind you of its spiritual purpose. This could be a candle, flowers or a crystal, for example. The ritual involved in lighting a candle, putting in fresh flowers, acknowledging a picture of one of the great spiritual leaders, can be very helpful to quieten the mind and prepare you for meditation. It also honours Spirit.

The reason why it is important to be regular and specific in your practice is that your Guides and Helpers in Spirit, described in Chapter Seven, will become accustomed to you meditating in a particular place at a particular time and will join you there spontaneously. Thus, communication with them will be much quicker and easier and your practice will be much more profound.

It is not necessary to sit cross-legged on the floor, though it is fine to do so if you like this technique. You may find it most effective to sit in an ordinary straight-back chair that is comfortable. Use an armchair if you wish, but ensure it is not so soft that you fall asleep! What is important is to be able to sit up with a reasonably straight (not rigid) spine so that your chakras are aligned. Please avoid lying down to meditate, unless you need to do so for health reasons.

If you find yourself saying, 'I can't meditate today because I can't find the time', explore this within yourself. If it is a one-off because you were up at 4 am to catch a plane and didn't get home until midnight the night before it would be understandable not to wish to rise at 6.30 am in order to sit for half an hour. In such circumstances, try and spend five or ten minutes in contemplation instead, perhaps before leaving home, raising your consciousness (see below) and connecting to Spirit.

If you find yourself regularly pushed for time, you may wish to ask if you are really committed to your spiritual growth or what is holding you back. Meditation is a fundamental aspect of spiritual development because it is the most important opportunity there is to align with your soul, to connect with Spirit and to create the future using the power of the mind. It can be difficult to get into the routine of regular meditation, but it is most helpful to do so. To begin with you may feel restless, edgy, filled with trivial thoughts and most unspiritual, but after a while of sitting (and it may be days, weeks or months) you *will* begin to feel more focused, in control, centred and connected. You will look forward to this time with anticipation and joy, and it will become a highlight of your day.

Spiritual journals

If you do any spiritual work, whether it is a daily meditation, a class, or any of the exercises in this or other books, it is very helpful to record your experiences in a spiritual journal. Any notebook will do, but I recommend, if you can, that you buy or ask to be given as a gift the most beautiful journal you can find to honour yourself and the work. Keep the book for your spiritual work only and make sure every time you make an entry that you date it, including the year. You will read it perhaps years later and be amazed by what you have experienced.

You may wish to keep either this or a separate journal by your bed to record your dreams. Similarly, some people keep a gratitude journal and record all that has happened in a day for which they wish to give thanks. It may be thanks for good weather, a safe journey, loving friends, an unexpected gift, or just for being alive on our wonderful planet. It is a lovely way to prepare for sleep.

A word about spiritual protection

Before I give you a meditation you may like to do every day, I will digress for a moment once again and talk about how you can shield yourself from negative energies that you may come across in your day-to-day living. Furthermore, it is particularly important to protect yourself when you are about to do a meditation, such as the one that follows, because as your chakras open and you are connecting to Spirit you are more sensitive than usual and so more vulnerable. Indeed, some people protect themselves every day or several times a day as a matter of routine, particularly if they are living in a city or interacting with large numbers of people where the energies are not always uplifting. Spiritual protection takes no time at all.

There are a number of methods available for protecting yourself and they are all very simple.

1. Surround yourself with golden light

See yourself covered by a sphere of white light and then imagine a thick layer of gold light being superimposed upon it. As a result, you have a beautiful but very tough spherical golden shell, like an egg shell, all around you. Anything harmful that touches that shell will bounce off it and nothing negative can reach you. The egg shell of light is Spirit.

2. Call upon your spiritual helpers

I explain who these are in Chapter Seven, and they include, for example, your guardian angel who is always by your side, but you can choose any helper you like. It can be a religious leader from your own religion or faith, God, or even an archetype such as Superman. Ask them to join you, and to protect you from all harm or negativity that may come your way.

3. Put the mantle of protection of Mother Mary around you

Many people, even those who are not Catholic or Christian, get great comfort from Her gentle but powerful presence. If you are drawn to do so, call to Mary mentally or out loud and ask Her to give you her mantle of Protection. Visualise Her coming behind you and placing around you Her cloak of blue. Feel Her hands pulling the cowl over your head, and fastening the cloak so that no part of your body is visible or exposed to anything unwelcome, including your feet and hands. You will feel safe and loved.

4. Use your power animals

A power animal is an animal that exists in the spiritual realms rather like an angel. (Again, power animals and angels are discussed at greater length in Chapter Seven.) Like angels there are one or two animals who are constantly with you, invisibly of course, to guard and look after you. Even if you do not know what species of animal they are, you can call in your power animals and ask them to guard and protect you actively from any harm or negativity. They do it anyway, even if you are unaware of them, but you will feel very safe if you know consciously they are with you and on alert.

5. Invoke the protection of God

Ask, mentally or out loud, for God and all Beings of Light to ensure your well-being at all times.

You can adjust these techniques to accommodate the terminology or religious practice with which you are comfortable. If you protect yourself regularly it will strengthen your sense of connection with the world of Spirit as well as help you deal with any baser energy you may encounter in your day-to-day activities or when you are spiritually open, such as in or following meditation.

The meditation that follows is very powerful and I ask you please to remember the importance of protecting yourself in the way you choose when you begin and at the end of it.

Exercise 1: A daily meditation practice for spiritual students

Preparation

Try to ensure you will not be disturbed for half an hour. It will be helpful to have a notebook and pen to hand, your spiritual journal, to record any impressions or messages.

Light a candle or incense if you wish.

Face East if you can, but don't worry if this is impractical. The Light of Spirit comes from the East and it is helpful to look towards it during meditation.

Sit with a straight but not rigid spine. Ensure both feet are firmly on the floor. Rest your hands comfortably in your lap, palms facing up or down as you choose.

Close your eyes and relax your body and take a few deep breaths. Check that your tongue is not tense – it often is without us realising it. Now put protection around yourself.

Alignment and visualisation

Focus on the root chakra, imagining a golden thread being drawn slowly from it up to the sacral chakra, to the solar plexus chakra, and then to the heart chakra, so you see them as in a line with each other like a jewelled belt.

Focus on the heart chakra. Visualise it as a golden flower unfurling its petals and expanding. Sense and feel your heart at the centre of the flower glowing with love, radiant with beauty. Spend about five minutes concentrating on your heart, visualising it opening up and getting bigger and bigger with all the love that is in it. Sense your love going out to all those you love and to mankind, and know that it is making the world a better place.

Leaving your heart open and still radiating forth love, slowly draw the golden thread, which is probably now much wider than when you started, from the heart chakra to the throat chakra and then to the third eye. Focus your attention on your third eye. (You may find it helpful to roll your eyes upwards under your eyelids, while keeping your eyes closed.) You may feel a physical sensation like a tiny headache in the area of your third eye, which will indicate that your consciousness is being raised.

Stay focusing on your third eye for a moment or two. If it becomes sore, relax and move your attention back to the heart. It will mean merely that you are not yet ready to do this part of the exercise for more than a moment. As you practise you will be able to sustain this focus for longer. Do not strain or overdo it and stop if the soreness persists.

Draw the golden thread up to the crown chakra. Visualise it once again as the golden jewelled belt linking all seven of the chakras and then see it moving out of the crown chakra towards a golden ball of brilliant light a little way above your head. This ball represents your soul. Try to send the golden thread upwards so that it merges with that golden ball that is your soul.

See yourself as a Being of Light aligned with your soul, knowing that you have raised your consciousness to the level of Light. Stay focused in this way for a minute or more (not more than five minutes) if you can. If your head at any time feels physically uncomfortable, then draw your attention back down to the heart chakra or stop altogether. This can be the result of over-concentration, which is why it is important to be relaxed, gentle and unhurried in this meditation.

This process so far is likely to take you ten minutes.

Meditation

Relax your focus from your soul back to your heart and then move outside yourself. Become the observer. Allow your mind to be open, receptive to any messages, images or sensations that may come to you. Watch how you breathe, if you feel any physical sensations in your body, if there is a noise or a scent around you. Watch and observe, *keeping your mind still*, focusing on the now. If everyday thoughts come into your mind, let them come through and out.

Make a note of any message that comes to you, even if you think you are just imagining what you are sensing or hearing. If you break off to make a note, resume your meditation where you left off.

This process will take about ten minutes.

Communication

Raise your consciousness to your crown chakra again and sense a clear channel, like an open pipe, moving from your crown upwards to where your spiritual helpers are waiting to communicate with you. Even if you cannot see them in your mind's eye (which you probably won't!) know that they are there. Ask, mentally or out loud, for them to join you. You may feel their energies around you as a warmth, perhaps a breeze, a shiver down your back – it is different for everybody and don't worry if you feel nothing at first. This is quite common.

Mentally or out loud greet them and thank them for joining you. If you have a problem you would like their advice on, ask them for help. Put the question, wait with an open relaxed mind and if you get an answer, however tentative it may be at first, write it down. (If no answer comes, wait for it to come in a more indirect way, perhaps in your dreams, in an article in a paper or from something someone says. Be alert, for it will come but sometimes in unexpected ways.)

If you have no question, ask them if they have anything to say to you – and see what impression comes to you. Sometimes you will get nothing, sometimes a message, sometimes just the sense of their energy about you, which can be very lovely.

You may wish to sit in silent communication during this third stage of the meditation, have a chat, ask for help or ask questions. You may choose. At the end of the time, thank them for being with you, say it is time to go but that you will be back tomorrow and would like them to be present again, or words to that effect.

Gently close down your chakras as suggested above, perhaps seeing them as flowers folding back into bud or shutters coming across them. Sense your aura, which will have expanded sometimes considerably, close to your body. Finally, ask that the mantle of protection of your Master, or Mary if you prefer, be placed around you for your complete protection. If you wish, surround yourself with light.

This phase also takes ten minutes.

Before you leave your sacred space, make a note of any impressions, images, symbols or sensations you have not already recorded. Leave the place with gratitude, serene but purposeful and ready for the day ahead.

Chapter One

What Does It Mean to Be Spiritual?

When the spiritual adventure which is now my life began with my fall that dark January night, I reacted like many people do whose soul has been awakened – I poured myself into spiritual exploration like an alcoholic seeking a bottle. Adopting a scattergun approach, I read avidly and perhaps indiscriminately, I learnt to meditate and spent hours doing so, I went on courses and workshops and underwent all sorts of healings and therapies. I was like a sponge; it was an excess of enthusiasm but it did me no harm and eventually most of the interests that were not appropriate for me fell away as I became more selective and more aware of myself and my needs as a spiritual being.

LEARNING THROUGH EXPERIENCE

An erroneous belief that I had during this early exploratory process was that I could not be spiritual without being taught how. One of my core spiritual understandings, explored in detail in Chapter Three, is that after we die we 'reincarnate', meaning that we will be reborn in a new body with a new personality and environment to live a new life of learning and experience. I know now that many, many lifetimes of spiritual service had left me with a latent seam of knowledge and understanding waiting to be recalled and used but, initially, I felt at the bottom rung of the spiritual ladder and that I knew nothing. If I knew nothing, I reasoned, then everyone else in the fascinating world of the New Age was 'better' than me. Furthermore, those advanced souls who called themselves 'Teacher', 'Master'[1], 'Guru' must be exalted people deserving of the highest respect and deference and perfect for helping me grow.

It took a while for the penny to drop. In those days I lived in Chorleywood just outside London and I took full advantage of my proximity to a large number of people describing themselves as evolved spiritual beings who had the gift to be able to accelerate the soul journey of seekers like me. I spent many hours and a lot of money lying on couches in incense-filled rooms listening to chants or meditations, being stroked or 'energised', and would usually leave feeling exactly the same as when I had arrived. Being a bit in awe of these gurus and having no confidence in my spiritual discernment I believed most of what they told me. One particular incident brought me to my senses.

Someone had told me about a very special and exclusive 'master' who had extraordinary powers to shift blocked energy through touch. Of course, I longed to meet him and work with him and was thrilled to speak to him and be invited to his home for a healing session. So, on a cold and wet February night I trudged across London to his home somewhere near Brixton. After a long and difficult journey I found his address and was surprised to find a dingy house in an insalubrious area with rubbish overflowing onto the street. One harsh light burned inside and there was no reply when I rang the bell, though I heard voices and movement. I called his number and again there was no reply. I waited thinking he had been held up and after a further 20 minutes decided to leave.

Having walked a little way I decided for some reason to return and this time heard voices and music. I could see through the window the 'guru' who was smoking what seemed to be a joint, drinking with friends and was clearly in no state to do a healing – if I had wanted it. I had a clear moment of truth, realising that he had forgotten I was coming, had hidden from me when I turned up and then had resumed his socialising when he thought I had gone – and that I did not feel comfortable about him at all.

So, I trudged home again having achieved nothing except a sense of relief that I had not had to enter what seemed to be an unclean and uninviting place to be alone with a stranger I felt uneasy about. The next day he called me and said he had been held up at another healing session that had over-run, could we reschedule? I declined.

WHAT IS A SPIRITUAL MASTER?

While the experience had been disappointing and tiring, like so many things that happen to us it taught me some valuable lessons. I learnt about spiritual honour and integrity and how it is lacking in evasiveness and lies. Anyone can make a mistake, forget an appointment, but what I witnessed and heard about him and how he lived dispelled all respect I might have had for this teacher. I realised that spiritual masters have to earn the title. It is not enough to make claims, to demand recognition and veneration; it is through their being and doing that they earn spiritual esteem. If someone, anyone, is arrogant, patronising, ego-driven, if their life is a total mess, where is the mastery, where is the example in that? A true master inspires. A true master demands nothing. A true master lives through love and understanding. A true master behaves with modesty and integrity. A true master never judges and always puts others first. A true master stands up for what he believes in. A true master encourages his or her students to become masters themselves, to be spiritually empowered, and is delighted to teach them all he or she knows.

A master, anyone who is spiritual in fact, has a personality and is

21

human with human frailties like everyone in the world. His child gets sick and he worries; the taxman pursues him and he gets frustrated. When Jesus visited the Temple and saw a sacred place that was intended for prayer being used by money lenders and pedlars, He got angry; and the Dalai Lama grieved to leave his dogs in Tibet when he was forced to flee. They felt and expressed emotion, but probably moved through it more rapidly and with more control than the majority of people. It is important that evolved teachers are seen to be human, accessible and approachable, not saints in a body. The same applies to you as a spiritual being. It is not necessary nor appropriate for you to try to suppress your personality 'warts and all' in order to be, or be seen as perfect, for every characteristic you have is there for a purpose, as you will see later in this book.

BEING SPIRITUAL

There are, nonetheless, certain qualities, attitudes and behaviour you can encourage in yourself to help you become more spiritual. For example, if you focus on trying to look saintly, you are focused on yourself and your appearance. This is ego. Someone who is spiritual always is considerate of others and doesn't care about their image – or even think about it. The expression 'having the heart in the right place' sums it up.

To be spiritual is a state of living and being; it is not a label which says 'I am spiritual'. It is very likely that if you are reading these words you are yourself spiritual, an evolved soul without necessarily knowing it consciously. Spiritual people are found in every walk of life and many of them would be amazed – perhaps horrified! – to be described as such. I know some and so do you. They may be family members, or part of your life in some other way, perhaps even quite remotely. Who do you sense loves their work and tries to do it to the very best of their ability? Who do you know who may be in a job that is difficult, but still they do their best? Who do you know who, despite everyday frustrations and problems, still manages to live with kindness and understanding? Who inspires you?

I spent 12 years working in the world of politics and, as a political lobbyist, met many politicians and got to know a number of them very well. Some, sadly, were and are clearly self-serving and motivated by a desire for power and political longevity. Even though they had entered that world most probably with good intentions, they were seduced by the trappings of status and influence. There were others who were and are driven genuinely by an aspiration to bring about change for the greater good and are prepared to give up everything they have in order to do what they believe to be right. This is altruism and altruism is being spiritual. On the bigger world stage, think of Nelson Mandela, Anita Roddick, Mother Theresa as examples of people fighting for what they believed in without thought for themselves.

Away from the world of politics and campaigning there are those who see themselves as 'ordinary' but who epitomise spirituality. I am blessed to have Kevin to help me with my wild and beautiful garden in Wales. Originally a glassblower, he knows as if by osmosis so much about wild flowers, birds, nature, horticulture, and he cherishes every living thing. A gentle, modest man, he loves and cares for his family and his environment, appreciates and contributes to our community, and for me is the personification of a good man, a spiritual person. He does his best, but I have a sense he sees himself as nothing special. He is.

Who do you know who has values like Kevin? I am referring here not necessarily to Kevin's specialist skills, rather to his compassion and good intentions. Is it your bin-man? Your assistant at the supermarket checkout? Your boss? The teacher of your child? Is it you?

THE PLACE OF RITUAL IN BEING SPIRITUAL

Spirituality is different for everyone and there is not one way only to be a spiritual person. I learnt through experience that what is a fruitful spiritual practice for one person may not necessarily be helpful to you or someone else and that it is up to each of you to find what suits you best. In the end, spirituality is innate and cannot be imposed, though a wise teacher can assist the process. It is already there at the heart of you, waiting to be accessed when you are ready.

While for me I prefer a practice which is as simple as possible, a number of people get great comfort from ritual and procedures such as affirmations, prayer, working with crystals, healing retreats or through organised religion, to give just a few examples. This is fine and they can be very beneficial and an important part of spiritual life. It is important, however, to see that these techniques are aids to your spirituality and not the means to spiritual unfolding in themselves. You may be drawn to a particular church because you find comfort in the rites and ceremonies involved, the familiarity of the order and routine, the sense of community that is engendered as well as the teachings and guidance available. Spirituality is at the heart of every religion even if it is expressed in different words and ways, but you don't have to belong to a faith in order to be spiritual.

The problem comes when you are more focused on the trappings and the surroundings than what lies beneath them; when the beliefs are imposed rather than deeply felt; when there is compulsion not spontaneity, rigidity of thought rather than freedom of expression; when the 'priest' becomes the intermediary between you and God, or the Source, rather than the facilitator for direct access; when aspects of power, control, even intimidation and fear are a corrosive part of a particular faith.

SPIRITUALITY AND RELIGION

All of you are aware of examples where a church or its representative has abused its power. The pages of history are filled with information about blood-stained wars waged in the name of religion, such as the Crusades, the massacres of the Cathars by the Pope's army, even the terrorist conflict in Northern Ireland. Priests from many traditions have used punishment and fear to control and subjugate for thousands of years, and churches still demand total obedience from their flocks in certain instances. Sometimes these priests believe genuinely that they are doing the will of God. Other individuals deliberately try to disempower their flock for financial gain, sexual gratification or otherwise to increase their authority. These people, by using their position as God's representative or spokesperson, are employing the most devious form of spiritual manipulation as well as reinforcing the belief among the masses that God is separate and distant from them.

There are, of course, many priests who throughout the ages to the present day have opposed divisiveness, corruption or malpractice and have lived and taught and died according to the highest spiritual precepts and conviction, an example and inspiration to all who care to see. Certain organised religions, too, encourage freedom of spiritual expression, connection and communication using loving compassion and kindness as the basis for their beliefs. Tibetan Buddhism is a remarkable example of spirituality in action.

THE TIBETAN SPIRITUAL EXPERIMENT

Hundreds of years ago Tibet made a decision to live as a spiritual and therefore peaceful nation. So, the country was ruled by the Dalai Lama, the head of the Tibetan Buddhist faith and the heart of the country was its religion. There was no army, no attempt to expand its borders, and a spiritual way of life based on that religion prevailed. So, when the Chinese invaded in 1950 there was no opposition not only because the Tibetans did not have the military means but also because they believed totally in harmony and acceptance.

Because Tibet has for so long been focused on being a spiritual nation, the people and the land itself exude spirituality in the same way that you take breaths all the time, without thinking about it. It is automatic and all-encompassing, embedded in the Tibetan psyche. There are not as many monasteries and temples now since the arrival of the Chinese, but still quite a few, and they are an important part of the local community. While there are priests and monks, their role is not to act as intermediaries and the people are encouraged and expected to pray and interact directly with their three Buddhas and the archetypal gods of their faith. So, even if the monks are praying or chanting in ceremony, anyone can enter the monastery and make a prayer or give offerings to the gods.

In Lhasa, the capital, there is a magnificent 1,000 year-old monastery called the Jokung Temple which is the Tibetan equivalent of Westminster Abbey. One evening I decided to go to the Jokung to hear the monks at their evening prayers. I was early, and as I waited for the great doors to open to let me in, I was joined by what became a huge crowd of Tibetans all chanting under their breaths the sacred prayer which is *Om Mani Pedme Hum*,[2] all excited and anticipatory as they thronged around awaiting the hour of entry. There were hundreds of people and when the doors opened they rushed in, not to hear the prayers of the monks, but to reach the shrine of the particular god to whom they had come to pray. It was like a football crowd waiting to get into Wembley for the Cup Final. What was amazing about this event, apart from the energy and devotion, was that the prayers take place every evening, not once a year, and so this happens every day.

Can you imagine this happening outside Canterbury Cathedral?

Unlike certain other religions, the practices of Tibet are joyful, which is what true spirituality is. They are a part of everyday life and are treasured. I visited the country not so long ago and was awed by the spiritual directness and simplicity that is endemic among the native people and in the land. Sadly, the Chinese who now control Tibet have outlawed many traditional spiritual practices including reverence for and recognition of the exiled Dalai Lama, but nothing can suppress the spirit of Tibet, and I found this demonstrated time and again.

THE KEYS TO BEING SPIRITUAL

Everyone, not just the Tibetans, can be spiritual. Indeed, I believe that everyone *is* spiritual but some people have forgotten, or don't care, what this means. At its deepest level, being spiritual means caring for the needs of your soul through your actions and this is what this chapter and indeed this book is all about. It is what you do in your everyday life that determines if and how far, how fast your soul and hence your spirituality will expand in your lifetime. I will explore this aspect of being spiritual in detail in Chapter Four.

So, at its core, being spiritual involves a way of living and being based on pragmatism. This is what Kevin has. He does not (as far as I know) think about his spirituality nor how to increase it, he just lives it, and that is fine. If he wanted to be more proactive about being spiritual, as you may do, there are simple techniques and practices that he and you could introduce into your lives involving self-awareness and behaviour as the basis for further spiritual growth. They are described below.

Good intent
Your actions, as I have said, determine your spirituality, and every action you take arises from an intention. There is nothing that you do, say, or think – these are all actions – that does not have an intention behind it. If your intention is pure and you are acting

from an ethos of integrity, this will help your spiritual or soul journey. If the intention is insincere, selfish or malicious then this will be a hindrance or impediment to that journey, with implications for your everyday life, which is the reflection of your soul.

An acquaintance of mine called Mary, from Surrey, became involved with a widower, John, who was a little pompous, perhaps, but he meant well. Over time she became irritated by his mannerisms and formality and ended the relationship in a rather unkind way, much to his bewilderment. He behaved with great discretion, however, and never mentioned her name except with courtesy. She, however, determined to humiliate him as much as she could and spread hurtful and untruthful stories about him, justifying her actions as wishing to warn and protect others from him. Mary's intention clearly was to do harm even though she pretended otherwise both to herself and to others, while well-meaning John wanted to do what was right.

It does not matter what the outcome of the action is, what matters is what lies behind it, though the outcome itself can be surprising. In the case of Mary and John, above, her standing in the community was diminished by her malice while he evoked sympathy and some admiration for his handling of the situation.

So, spiritual intention includes generosity of thought and deed, compassion for everyone and everything, and helping others when you can. In other words, you try to do your best always and genuinely.

Why don't you have a little look at your own life, just for a moment? Sometimes it is the small events that are most indicative of where you stand regarding your intention and therefore your level of spirituality.

In another case, a neighbour of mine, Vanessa, rushed home early from work in order to help her frail mother get to hospital. Her intention was excellent, but sadly, in her hurry, she had an accident just outside her home, colliding with another car as she turned in. Fortunately no one was hurt, but she was unable to get her mother to her appointment because of the delay that ensued and the damage done to her car.

Vanessa was very upset by what had happened and blamed herself, even though no harm came to her mother. It took a long time for her to see that, because her intention had been pure, based on kindness and love and the wish to be of help to her mother, she had done nothing wrong. It was spirituality in action, coming from the heart, and unlike in Mary's case it was genuine.

- If you are serving up a meal for your family, how far do you look after yourself and your plate first? Is it your intention to have the choicest cuts, the biggest portion for yourself, or is it to be fair, or is it to give the best to those you love, lovingly?

- If you are watching television with your partner, which of you insists on watching 'your' programmes? How often do you control the remote? How often do you argue about it? Why?

- If you are reading about the misfortunes of a celebrity, how far is your interest salacious or prurient? Why are you reading it? Is it your intention to enjoy their humiliation? Do you feel any compassion for them?

- If you have an insurance claim for, say, lost baggage, would you inflate it to get more money? So, is it, then, your intention to deceive, to steal? Or is your intention to get back a return for all the insurance premiums you have paid over the years? If so, either way it is still theft.

- If a bumble bee flies into your room and buzzes round making lots of irritating noise, do you try and let it out, kill it or leave it to die? Is your action coming from a place of compassion? (It is important to remember that all living creatures deserve to be treated with respect, however small, and if you have the choice of behaving compassionately or thoughtlessly, the former is always preferable.)

- If you find a £20 note in the back of a taxi, what would you do with it? Honestly.

- When was the last time you gossiped about someone behind their back? Was the intention loving? Would you have said it in exactly the same way to their face?

- If a frail old lady in front of you is slow at the checkout and holds you up, do you mentally grumble and complain or do you offer to help her with her unloading and packing instead?

It may be that one or two of these examples will feel familiar to you. All of them are common situations to do with love, kindness, compassion, selflessness, greed and self-centredness. They are reminders of how easy it is for your intention to become tainted and of the importance of being aware of the intention behind everything you think or say or do. They are reminders also that the way you live your life is a clear demonstration of your level of spirituality.

If you catch yourself with an impure intention then change it immediately! It is remarkable how switching your intention alters the energies to do with that situation and how you feel – and often the outcome as well. Changing meanness and lies to generosity and integrity, and meaning it, is truly balm to the soul. So, hand round your favourite chocolates, buy the first round of drinks, make that overdue phone call to your elderly relative, don't pretend to be ill to get a day off work, pay what you owe cheerfully and so on! The kindness and honesty you give out will return to you as blessings many times over.

I know, it is not so easy to do as for me to say it! In my life, time and again I have caught myself potentially 'letting myself down' in this regard and while I am better at seeing, anticipating where my intention is wandering or wavering and catching it just in time, even now old habits return to remind me of what I teach.

Being non-judgemental

Talking about intentions reminds me also about judgement and how very important it is not to judge or criticise yourself or others. There was a time when I languished in a sea of negative thought and memories. If I went on a long train journey, for instance, I would pass the hours going over in my mind the many times when I had said or done words or deeds which were embarrassing or shameful, certainly hugely to be regretted, I thought. I lashed myself with recollections going back to when I was three years old, remembering situations that made me wince.

In fact, nothing I did was very bad at all, just human really, and the people to whom I had expressed myself clumsily, for example, would have forgotten it within minutes if they had noticed it at all. I did not forget, but judged myself as flawed extremely effectively. So, I would arrive at my destination feeling an abject failure after all my negative introspection. My subconscious intention had been to punish myself and I did it very well. Every time I looked back at myself this way my shame at my mistakes grew stronger.

This was a number of years ago before I found myself spiritually, and when I started to see beyond my internal misery, to think about the bigger picture, one of the first things I did was to consciously look at how much I judged myself (and always negatively) and to stop doing so. Because I was so deeply into self-judgement, I also realised that I was very good at judging others, again usually negatively, and that this was not useful either. So I changed.

It took time but when I saw how corrosively judgement had affected me I did all I could to reverse a pattern of behaviour that had been with me nearly all my life. If I found myself going back into the past, starting to brood about what I had done before, I refused to go on with it. I ordered my mind (the instigator in all of this) to be quiet and distracted it with something else that was positive or otherwise constructively occupying. It became easier after a while and I began to understand how everything we experience, however negative it may seem at the time, is for a reason, a purpose to help us grow as spiritual beings. If this is so, then judgement and criticism of anyone is a waste of time and hugely unhelpful. Instead we must try to accept everybody and every situation with understanding and sensitivity and as an opportunity to learn and grow.

Judgement creeps in easily and it is important to be alert to it. You can find yourself judging the quality of a piece of homemade cake ('The fruit has sunk, I could do better'), someone's appearance ('My goodness, she has put on weight'), a star's morals ('I reckon she sleeps around a lot') and so on. Much modern journalism is judgemental and feeds the opinions of its readers or audience negatively, sometimes to the point of evoking mass hysteria. Whenever you think or speak ill of someone it impacts upon your spirituality and also upon the target of your criticism, as you will see later.

Please remember that there is a difference between judgement which is critical or subjective and 'good' judgement which is discernment based on clear fact. If, for example, you saw a young child playing with matches your reaction would be to see the potential danger and to remove them. This would be acting with good judgement.

The power of thought

The mind is an incredibly powerful tool to shape how you live your life and so how you are as a spiritual person. Your thoughts create your environment, your state of mind, your success, your fears, your abundance and how you behave. You see, what you think about and how you feel about it creates itself, even magnifies itself. So, if you are fearful, the more you worry the more likely it is you will manifest what you fear. If you are positive and confident about a situation, the more likely it is for that situation to have a happy outcome.

A client of mine, Jack, had a dog he worshipped. He had no family and the dog was his world. Even though the dog was quite young it became ill and, while the diagnosis was uncertain, it looked very serious and the vet was pessimistic. Jack, however, was determined to do all he could to help his dog live: he prayed and also refused to think about the worst that could happen, focusing instead on the idea that his pet would recover fully. To the amazement of everybody the dog pulled through and lived for many years more.

Of course, a positive approach does not always bring about the outcome you want, but it is much more likely to do so than fearing the worst.

Let me demonstrate how changing your thoughts can change your life and spiritual well-being. I have a friend called Sue. Sue is also on a spiritual path and she can be a little over-sensitive about it. For years she had an obsession with noise. She wanted to have total silence around her so that she could meditate and do her spiritual practices (of which there were many) to best effect. Living just outside Watford and near Heathrow this was not easy for her and she complained a lot about the disturbance and the difficulties this caused her. Then new neighbours moved in who decided to do a lot of rebuilding to their property, with associated noise. Sue worked from home and became increasingly upset by the amount of disruption coming from next door and all around her, monitoring it, complaining about it and fighting it. The more she tried to stop it the worse it got, until she realised one day that she had to deal with the situation another way.

She made a conscious effort to accept the right of the neighbour to create a beautiful home for his family in accordance with his intention to support them lovingly. She tried to get on better terms with him and came to see how his home improvements would benefit the value of her property. She learnt techniques to insulate the sound away from her, so that in the end she was hardly aware of all the noises around and her quality of life and peace of mind improved considerably. She recognised that, if she thought about the noise constantly with anger or distress, that noise or disturbance was going to increase until she learnt to accept it or ignore it. When it no longer mattered to her, when it was no longer energised by her negative thinking, it went.

Detachment

What Sue did with her difficulty over noise, what I did with my issues to do with self-judgement, what *you* can do when you think you have negativity somewhere in your life, is to learn to detach from your emotions and fears. When you feel apprehension or anxiety, anger or guilt, remember that these feelings are created by the mind and that they will inhibit your level of spirituality. The mind is like a chatterbox, constantly reminding you of 'what-ifs' and possibilities that may never happen, reviewing the past and looking to an unknown future and usually seeing the negative in everything. It is a form of control over you and if you are not careful an unquiet, restless mind can dominate you totally at the expense of your spiritual purpose and peace of heart. Meditation can be very helpful to bring about a quiet mind, but it is still important for you to learn to be the observer of your words, deeds, thoughts and intentions so that you can switch from negative to positive as soon as you are aware of the need so to do.

Detachment does not mean passivity or coldness. I am not talking about detaching from our society and closing yourself off – far from it. Detachment means being able to stand back and see yourself, others, world events, with compassion and understanding, with no judgement. You are still part of the world, working and interacting, loving and sharing, enjoying what you have, but you are doing so at a different level of consciousness. You are doing it from your spiritual self and at this point your mind is working beautifully in co-operation with that self and all is well.

Cosmic awareness

Self-awareness, then, is a critical part of being spiritual, but your understanding of yourself goes beyond who and what you are as a personality in a human body. Through your soul, which has no boundaries, you are part of the cosmic totality, part of everything that exists in space, and if you can see and feel that cosmic inter-connectedness you can maximise all of your spiritual potential, leading you to a state and a place of bliss. More importantly, you can, if you wish, through this expansion of vision, strengthen your connection with God. I will look at your cosmic connections in much more detail in Chapter Seven on Our Spiritual Helpers and Chapter Four, The Soul's Journey.

Honouring nature

This interconnectedness applies closer to home also, to the rocks and minerals and all the creatures and living beings that share the planet with you and in countless instances provide you with the means for life on Earth.

There is little regard, kindness, consideration or respect for the other forms of life that exist alongside us, even though this approach is a vital part of being spiritual. In many parts of the world people believe that everything exists for their pleasure or benefit, that man is the most important species and anything to help humanity's survival, expansion and comfort is acceptable, at whatever cost to other living beings. They have forgotten that we are no better nor more important than anything else that lives and that we have a responsibility to ensure the well-being of the other components of nature's scheme, as well as our own.

This selfish attitude has prevailed for years and as a result a serious imbalance has resulted whereby there are too many humans using increasingly scarce resources without heed for where this will lead. It is ironic that it is the bulk of humanity that has forgotten its divine source and spiritual purpose which is motivated by selfishness and materialism and so has so much to learn and heal, while the world of nature is pure in intention and deed and has never forgotten its part in the greater scheme of God.

Consider how much in balance is this world beyond us, despite the predations of man, how the plants, the birds, the insects, the animals are part of a wonderful and perfect hierarchy in which they live according to their needs and the needs of those with whom they co-exist. For many thousands of years man was part of this harmonious system of balance, understanding and respect, and I believe will be again, if humanity is prepared to learn from its mistakes and be part of the whole once more.

Look around you from time to time, look closely and observe the wonders of nature. Listen to the birdsong, watch the trees, feel the earth beneath your feet and give thanks for the gifts of beauty, companionship and life these wonders give us.

Our pets and domestic animals are an important part of this natural system and can be a significant part of your spiritual and everyday life just as another human can be. For those of you who may wish to know more about the spirituality of animals, I include a brief explanation on page 66.

THE BENEFITS OF LIVING SPIRITUALLY

Many busy people in today's world would like to be more spiritual but think it would be too time-consuming and difficult, particularly if their lives are filled already with work, parenthood, financial responsibilities, stress and the general pressures of life in the twenty-first century. I hope I have demonstrated that being spiritual is an attitude and way of life that can become a fulfilling and automatic part of your practical existence. It does not have to be onerous, indeed, it should be a joy.

If you are able to become more aware of what it means to be a spiritual being, and to practise in the ways I have described, it will without question bring, at least, peace of mind, a loving appreciation of yourself and those around you, a sense of harmony, freedom from fear and anxiety, and an ability to shape your life as you would wish it to be.

You may find as you awaken to your spiritual calling that you want to be more proactive and introduce specific spiritual study and practices into your life in order to accelerate your opportunities for soul growth. If so, the information, guidance and practical exercises provided in *Spiritual Wisdom* will be of benefit.

If you wish to take your sense of spiritual purpose further it will lead you to God. Yes, I know some people feel close to the Great Creator already and you may feel your connection is perfect. That is wonderful but rare, and instead you may be one of many people who have a sense that something is missing in your life, it is a bit unsatisfactory, that it could be better – and I am making these comments to *you*.

You see, by practising your spirituality in the way I have described you are connecting to your highest self, which is the part of you which is true pure spirit, which is divine. By connecting to the divine you are connecting to God, the Source, and it is this innate connection that has been missing or forgotten for so many of you for so long. It is this that you as a spiritual being longs for and I will look at this in depth in the Chapter Four on The Soul's Journey.

SPIRITUALITY IN ACTION

So, at this point it may be helpful to summarise what it means to be spiritual:

- Think of others before yourself.

- Always have the best possible intentions in thoughts, words and action.

- Offer a helping hand whenever you see the opportunity.

- Do your best, always.

- Be discerning, with compassion.

- Learn to observe yourself, other people and world events with detachment.

- Do not be judgemental of yourself or others.

- Accept you may make mistakes and see them as opportunities to grow.

- Have kindness and respect for all life.

- Remember that you are part of a cosmic and divine totality. As such your potential is limitless.

Meanwhile, I don't want you to feel daunted by the advice I have given you so far! It does not mean you have to live a life of austerity or joylessness! Far from it. My intention is to assist you to enjoy your life and soul's journey as much as possible and for it to be as free from bumps and wrinkles as possible.

So, don't take yourself too seriously and learn to laugh when the unexpected happens, when you find yourself repeating the same pattern AGAIN. See everything that occurs as being an important part of your path even if you can't see the bigger meaning immediately and remember that you are not expected to have to live as a saint! You are an individual with a personality that is perfect for your purpose of being on Earth, and that includes having idiosyncrasies and frailties unique to you and which exist to teach you and the other people who are part of your life.

Exercise 2: Review, understand and amend your intentions and actions

The purpose of the exercise is to review and explore your intentions and actions of the day, to identify how far they were motivated by kindness and how you might have acted differently to make the day as positive and beneficial, spiritually, as possible.

The habitual practice of this exercise will enable you to understand the nature of your intentions in order for you to become more aware of your spirituality. Regular use will assist you to become more self-aware and will encourage compassion and altruism in everything you do.

I suggest you read through these guidelines at least once so that you are clear about what you will be doing before you begin the exercise.

Ensure, if you can, you do not do the practice if you are very tired or have been taking drinks or stimulants.

The exercise

Ahead of time, determine clearly when you will begin and for how long, if you wish it to be for a limited period only. It would be good to do it for a week at least, and the longer you can do it the more effective it will be.

Before you go to bed, when your day's activities are over and you are unlikely to be disturbed, turn your attention to the intention you have set for this exercise, which is that you will be reviewing the day that has just gone in the context of your intentions to the best of your ability. Forget about other things that may be on your mind such as what you have got to do tomorrow.

Now, think about the day you have just experienced:

- Review what you have felt, said, thought or done during the day and with what intention. What stands out?

- Consider without judgement how far everything you did was kind and of good intention. Where you have been negative, mentally replay the act or thought to make it positive and loving – from the heart.

- See how this feels.

Notice if there is a particular person or situation that has been a part of your day, and that always evokes a particular response from you. Consider why that is. If it is a negative response, try to change it.

Have your spiritual journal (described in the Introduction) to hand and make a record of anything particularly striking, or of any patterns that you may notice.

Go to sleep in the knowledge you have done all you can to put right any negative or unhelpful actions or intentions and that you have done your best.

Chapter Two

Karma

A consistent theme of this book is that everything you do, say or think affects your ability to progress as a spiritual being. It impacts your work, your relationships, your health, your finances, your overall well-being – the whole of your life and every part of your life, at all levels. This is karma, the Universal Law of Cause and Effect (the Universal Laws are discussed in Chapter 8). By understanding the true meaning and implications of karma, learning how to reduce negative karma and increase good karma, you will find your spiritual consciousness expanded and your approach to your life profoundly altered. It will truly change your life.

WHAT IS KARMA?

Karma is the record of all your thoughts, words and actions experienced in any lifetime. The reason why your karma is so very important is that when you do or say or think something, however trivial it may be, it triggers an effect (under the Universal Law of Cause and Effect) and that effect will impact your soul. So, if you think about it, you are changing your karma all the time. If you do something negative, your negative karma will increase. If you do something kind, it will increase the level of light on your soul because you will have created positive karma.

The intention is to achieve an equilibrium, so that if you record a karmic negative it is balanced out by a positive until eventually there are no negative karmic 'specks' on your soul at all and all that is left is light. Karma is not a punishment for what you have done wrong, it is a neutral balance sheet and it is the opportunity to learn and move forward as a spiritual being.

Your soul is a direct reflection of your karmic record both in this lifetime and previous lifetimes on Earth, which is why karma is so important. Remember, it is on Earth, when you are in incarnation, that you are able to make decisions, to have free choice about what you do in that incarnation and so you have direct control about if and how far you wish to allow your soul to expand. A lifetime on Earth, therefore, is a wonderful opportunity to change the balance of your karma and by this I mean to change how much light there is upon your soul. One of the reasons why our planet is a popular destination for souls is because it allows us to choose, learn and grow more rapidly than anywhere else in our universe. While spiritual growth occurs between incarnations, usually it is much slower.

Whatever you do has a karmic reaction and the karma reflects itself upon the soul as lightness or darkness. The more light there is upon the soul, the more evolved you are. If you do something to create 'good' karma, the light is there for ever. If you do something that is negative, then it is like a speck of dust that falls upon a clean work surface, it needs to be wiped away. The more specks of dust there are upon your soul, the more work you have to do in your everyday life through your thoughts and deeds to clean them up. The accumulation can become so weighty it is difficult to clear, and it can take many lifetimes and much effort to do so. Conversely, the more good karma you have, the easier it becomes to attract more – which will also help the release of your negative karma. So, good karma is permanent, negative karma can be and must be removed if the soul is to progress on its journey (this will be discussed in greater detail in Chapter Four).

Where the negative actions are minor then it is quite easy – if you are aware of what is going on – to clear the negative karma quickly, and indeed the sooner you are able to do so the better it is for your soul. So, if you have lost your temper with someone, the sooner you can apologise for it the better it is for you. If you have gossiped unkindly about a friend or colleague, then you may make amends by mentally apologising to them, with sincerity, and perhaps saying to those people who were sharing the gossip that you regretted having done so. Spiritual growth leads, inevitably, to greater self-awareness, and I know a number of people who become annoyed with themselves for occasional unkind thoughts or judgement. It is because they have so much light upon their soul that they are able instantly to see and feel a negative act, and it pains them almost physically. Their understanding and regret clears the karma immediately, and no harm is done.

The specks of karmic dust upon your soul will be different from each other. One might be the result of being rude to someone perhaps, another an overwhelming desire for that new handbag that you can't afford and don't need, and yet another lie in an insurance claim. If you reflect on your day or week (and this is why the exercise in the last chapter is so helpful) and find that you have incurred quite a few karmic specks don't judge yourself and find yourself guilty for those negative acts: instead, accept them as having happened as a way for you to learn about yourself and your life, mentally apologise to everyone affected and determine not to repeat them if you can help it. Then move on.

Sometimes life is so busy you become too engrossed in keeping up with your schedule to think about your actions and it can be helpful from time to time to do a little check on what you have been doing recently. When you do a karmic check-up, remember to include your intentions in your considerations. You may be surprised to find that what you thought was a big speck of dust was good karma after all.

Suzanne, a client of mine for many years, has an only son who was addicted to heroin. After trying counselling, gentleness, giving him money, food and shelter without any effect on his habit, she realised that he needed tough love. She reported him to the police for stealing from her, booked him into rehab and told him she would have no contact with him until he was totally clean, even if he were in serious trouble. She felt huge emotions of guilt, sadness and anger and told me she felt she was accruing lots of karmic dust through being so hard and unfeeling towards her beloved son.

It took many years of separation and hard experience, but eventually he gave up drugs and crime and became a drugs adviser to schools in his local community. His relationship with his mother has never been the same, however, though it continues to improve slowly.

In this case, Suzanne had done all she could to help him, throughout, and ultimately it was for him to choose how to lead his life. Because her intention was pure she incurred only positive karma as a result of her actions.

KARMA OVER LIFETIMES

An ideal situation would be to live a lifetime in which you incurred much good karma from your intention and wish to do your best and in which any negative karma you incurred was cleared by the time you died. Unfortunately it doesn't always happen that way and sometimes the impact of what you have done carries over to be cleared in the next life, or the next, or over many lifetimes. I am talking here not of minor human actions like shouting at a nurse, out of character, because you are frightened and in pain as death approaches, but behaviour or attitudes that are more harmful, or felt by the soul to be so. There is no graded list of what is best or worse karma, it is different for everybody. One person may have developed a pattern of extreme bullying (which could include shouting at nurses!), another may have been profligate with money and another may have been very selfish. Our karmic pattern is unique for each one of us. One of the reasons you reincarnate is to deal with old karma once and for all in order to assist the expansion of your soul. This is addressed in detail in the next chapter.

Over different lifetimes, patterns of behaviour or emotion become established and these can be very difficult to change. If you have been through a cycle of incarnations where you have been learning about poverty and hardship, you may have karmic issues to heal concerning your self-belief and right to abundance. Your spiritual helpers will give you everything you need to remind you of the lessons you are here to learn and if you do not see the opportunities or if you choose not to address them, then in the next lifetime you will return to address them again. You will not be able to progress on your spiritual journey until you have passed each test of learning.

Not only that, the intensity of the lesson will increase in each lifetime until the karmic lesson becomes so painful it is easier to give in and deal with it rather than resist. It is a bit like toothache: if you ignore it and hope it will go away it is likely to get worse and eventually you come to realise that the pain of being in the dentist's chair is better than the pain of the tooth. So it is with karma. For example, if you are someone who always has been supported by the state, family or community as the result of many incarnations as a monk or a nun, it can be terrifying to be forced to consider becoming responsible for your financial and physical well-being and that of your family.

A client of mine, Martha, was in exactly that situation. An intelligent woman from a middle-class background, she was a university student for as long as possible, living on grants and family handouts, until she met her partner and had two children. Neither of them worked, despite having good academic qualifications, and they claimed the state benefits available to people in hardship to give them what they needed to live.

There was never any money and when some came their way from occasional inheritances it was spent immediately so that they were back in their comfort zone of financial dependency. They did not like money, it made them uncomfortable, and while they worried about their precarious financial situation they preferred it to self-sufficiency.

I worked with Martha, using a form of past life regression that I have developed with a combination of guided visualisation and channelling. Through this we discovered that that they had had many experiences together of being beggars, monks, lunatics, slaves, and that this community dependency was a shared pattern for them. The understanding of this background to her life, and the release of the karma associated with it, created the breakthrough she had been seeking, and she was able to begin to move forward away from her dependency.

At this point in her life, Martha's partner died of alcoholism. Instead of running away from the situation, she determined to do something with her life. When she was approached to do counselling in her son's school, she took up the opportunity, and then more opportunities to work came her way. Old habits die hard, as they say, and she did not declare her new income at first, but questions began to be asked.

In the end it became so difficult to try to justify retaining her benefits and hiding her fee income that she decided that it would be easiest to be totally independent, for the first time in many lifetimes. It was a huge breakthrough, and changed her life. She had not realised she had been perpetuating an old karmic habit for all her life until then; now she is relishing her freedom and her success.

SELF-INFLICTED KARMA

When you are thinking about karma, please remember that if your intention is good you cannot incur negative karma. Similarly, if you are on Earth to have a particular set of human experiences, so long as you don't go too far beyond what was intended you will not incur negative karma either. If it is decided, for example, that in this lifetime you will learn what it is like to be a prostitute, using your body for money in order to nurture your children, there will be no karmic repercussions – unless you change the intention behind the learning.

So, if you neglect your children instead of feeding them because you don't care about them; if you use the money for drink and drugs and self-gratification instead; if the nature of the work becomes perverted because you choose not to say no; if you bring the 'work' home with you to the detriment of your children's welfare, all this can create negative karma for your soul and will inhibit your light unless it were part of the Plan for your Earth learning, created long before you were born. This Plan, or blueprint, for your life is explained in detail in the next chapter.

Conversely, some people who have incurred no significant karmic dust in a particular lifetime perceive themselves, nonetheless, to have erred and judge themselves for it. The judgement can perpetuate itself just like negative karma through successive lives and similarly needs to be cleared. This can occur for more evolved souls in particular, where their sensitivity and commitment to their spiritual journey can make them self-critical to the detriment of their soul's progress.

DOES KARMA AFFECT EVERYBODY?

Karma exists to help the soul, in other words to help you grow as a spiritual being. If your soul is asleep then whatever you do will not affect it and negative karma does not accrue. Conversely, acts of kindness and good intention can help a sleeping soul to awaken. (This is explained in Chapter Four, The Soul's Journey.)

Occasionally I have visions of some of my past lives. In one, I saw that I had a lifetime many hundreds of years ago when I was a young girl, a sacred dancer and bride to Krishna in a temple in India. I had been selected for this special role at a very young age and strict rules governed my conduct and lifestyle, one of which was to have no contact with any man, not even my father or brothers. Anyway, I fell in love with a handsome man who visited the temple. It was unilateral, we had no physical contact and he had no idea of how I felt. However, my sense of shame was immense for I felt I had violated all my vows to Krishna and had betrayed my God by my improper thoughts. I killed myself in my anguish, and while there was no actual karma involved in my learning another aspect of love, it took several lifetimes to heal my guilt and move on.

In certain parts of the world vicious acts of brutality are carried out by rebel armies or factions sometimes against their own people. Often they are described as 'mindless' acts, and this is what they are likely to be – deeds perpetrated by people, sometimes children, who themselves may have been abused, starving, fighting for survival, brainwashed into not thinking nor caring about what they are doing. They are on autopilot, out of control and following the destructive group mentality of which they are a part. They are killing, raping, torturing machines separated from heart, soul and spirit, and so their deeds have no karmic impact upon their dormant spiritual state.

Occasionally one or two of these fighters will try to resist the extremity of violence in order to limit the suffering of the victims, and any such act of compassion will spark a spiritual response and this is wonderful. As soon as you start to be aware of the impact of your words and actions, when you know the difference between right and wrong, when you begin to think of others beyond yourself, when you are kind and loving, then the soul begins to stir and your karmic learning can begin. It is the beginning of the soul's journey forward.

In the paragraphs above I have been speaking mainly of a group mentality when referring to mass slaughter and brutality or even natural catastrophes, both among the perpetrators and the victims. However, there are individuals in positions of authority who commit outrageous crimes against their people and the world by deliberate acts of callousness and cruelty for their personal gain. This is apparent in certain developing countries but is evident in the West too, where some politicians and directors of large companies put their desire for power and money above probity, responsibility, foresight and care. In such cases, if they are being over-zealous in applying their scheduled lessons about corruption or deception or power, if they are reinforcing rather than clearing old karmic patterns from past lives, or if they are initiating new unintended patterns, then they will incur negative karma on their soul and their opportunities for spiritual expansion will be inhibited.

Do not judge them. Their actions and example are great teachers in themselves, and you do not know how far they are great souls working to help us learn by their example, or whether they are misguided souls caught up in the world of matter.

While it can be distressing in the extreme to be a direct or vicarious witness to catastrophe and horror, I encourage you always to try to see the bigger picture. Every individual who is among the masses involved in wars, famines, gas chambers or other devastation, suffering, dying or killing is, as a soul, in that situation voluntarily, even if consciously they are not aware of it, for it is part of the Plan that was created, with their soul agreement, before they were born. It is an opportunity for them to begin or to resume the learning process of Earth school and to clear their karma, but, more significantly, their participation in dramatic world events also enables you, me and the rest of the world to see the depths of human depravity, thoughtlessness and selfishness, the antithesis of love, and to say, 'That is enough. No more.' Then the world can come back into balance and the new golden age of spirituality can begin. We may not like what occurs, but we have much to thank these brave souls for.

KARMIC RELATIONSHIPS

When there is a particularly traumatic event in a past life which leaves a karmic imprint, very often another person is involved and there is unfinished business between you. When this occurs you may both, when planning your next incarnations, decide to create the opportunity to finish that unresolved business and to clear the karma between you. If you do not you will both have to reincarnate for lifetime after lifetime until you have resolved the issue together.

Every person you have any connection with in your life is there for a reason, perhaps to clear karma or to remind you of your lessons in this lifetime or both. It may be to help you on your spiritual journey even if you have not 'met' before. This applies to your biological family, to your friends, to your colleagues, many of whom will have kept you company through many lifetimes. Your mother may have been your brother, hunting companion, cousin, daughter. Your husband may have been your work rival, your son, your teacher, and so on. These relationships do not have to be karmic, where there is an unresolved issue or debt between you from the past or present, but can quite simply be based on love. It is not necessary to know the past lives you have had together, indeed, it is not always helpful to focus on the past out of mere curiosity when there is the present to enjoy. Psychic insight or past life regression carried out by a professional is of benefit when you are in a situation that is causing you particular difficulty or stress.

There may be a pattern to all your karmic relationships and often it is one to do with power and control in some form or other. Just as you yourself can get into a karmic cycle which keeps you trying to learn the same hard lesson again and again, so it can happen between two people or even a family group that you both or all of you come into a lifetime to resolve a particular karmic issue between you that has been going on endlessly. The intention is always that in each lifetime through your mutual efforts and learning you will have a clear balance sheet between you at the end of it, but this does not always happen.

Some years ago I applied to work for an organisation in central London. At my final interview my future co-directors were invited to be present. One of them, John, whom I had not met before, arrived late for the meeting and without apology, unkempt, coat, coffee and croissant in hand, and from the outset was clearly determined to ensure I did not get the position. To the embarrassment of his colleagues he was exceedingly rude and his anger towards me was evident. I got the job nonetheless and from the start he did everything possible to undermine my position and to drive me out.

It took me years and hindsight to realise that he had done me a great favour. We had been together before in situations where we had been competitors and rivals in business, normally good-natured sometimes one winning, sometimes the other. Overall it was a balanced situation. In a particular incarnation, however, his jealousy went further than intended and he killed me. This was karmic. We returned together to clear the karma, but the next time he abused me mercilessly – and so it went on. So, we kept on coming back, he wanting to suppress me still and I was allowing him to take my power.

Coming together in this lifetime, in this work situation, enabled me to hold my power against aggressive masculinity as represented by him for the first time for many lifetimes and enabled him to learn to respect me again. I am grateful to him for helping me heal my karmic relationship with him and to reclaim my sense of self and equality in a male world.

People often come together in a relationship to resolve a particular karmic issue and when that is done they can choose whether to allow the relationship to continue or whether to part, the job completed. If you have been in a partnership that has been particularly painful, it may be there was a catalyst which caused one or other of you to decide to end it. Making the decision, taking control of the situation, can be exactly what is needed to balance the karma between you.

If you are in a difficult relationship situation now, whether it is at work or within your family, have a look at the patterns within that relationship and see if it could be karmic. If it is, then one of you needs to do something to redress the karmic imbalance, otherwise it will continue to perpetuate itself within this lifetime or the next.

Miriam is a lovely lady in many ways, self-assured and elegant, but she is also someone who had a difficult relationship with her mother. Being with her would leave her feeling inadequate, unwanted and unloved. She discovered that the two of them had had many lives together and that for the past three lives she had been the son, the daughter and the niece to her. In each of those three lifetimes she had died, been abandoned or been grossly neglected by her mother and this had created karmic guilt for her mother. So, it was the intention in Miriam's present life for her mother to nurture her successfully to adulthood and for Miriam's hurt and low self-esteem to be healed.

When Miriam saw beyond her own feelings she was able to recognise how much her mother had tried to be a good parent, despite many obstacles. She could see the patterns in her life that were there to remind them both of the issues to be addressed, and she understood that much of her hurt was past life memory rather than real. By looking beyond her subjective emotions and seeing her mother's position too, past and present, she was able to forgive the unintended or misinterpreted slights and to mend their relationship and, by so doing, heal the karma between them.

A number of clients have come to me with a similar story to each other. They met their spouse and both felt a strong attraction to each other and, even though there were warning signs about temper, irresponsibility and cruelty, they married. After sometimes years in an abusive relationship, something happened which was the last straw and they found the courage to walk out. In every case there was a strong karmic history between them and breaking the link decisively was what was necessary to clear it.

KARMIC VOWS

As part of your soul learning it is very likely that you have had lives which involved taking a vow or oath, or very occasionally even incurring a curse. Rituals of this sort have a profound impact upon your soul and you can incarnate time and again with the soul memory of these vows influencing your life significantly. You may be happy to keep some vows, such as a vow of integrity, but other vows may be obsolete and holding you back on your spiritual and temporal journey. It may be, indeed, that you are unaware of how many and what vows are impacting you still. It can be helpful to do an exercise to remove unwanted vows and oaths and one is given at the end of this chapter. In cases where the vow is deeply entrenched, it may be necessary to undertake past life regression therapy or other forms of healing to identify and remove it.

Vows can affect you in a number of ways.

A monastic or religious vow

As a monk, priest or nun in the Christian faith you will have taken solemn vows of chastity, poverty and obedience, and similar pledges will have been taken if you were serving in any religion. If you have difficulties in your sexual relationships, in finding and holding onto money or luxuries, in seeing yourself as a leader or with any sort of power, then it may well be that you are still subconsciously affected by old religious vows you took hundreds of years ago. You may feel a sense of guilt concerning these areas of your life now.

Marriage vows

The vow of marriage is still taken seriously by many people, as it has been since the institution of marriage began. Your connection with your partner or spouse may be ancient, going back to a time when marital obedience and fidelity was demanded absolutely if you were a woman, and when any other sort of behaviour could have caused the loss of your life. The influence of an old marriage vow ('worship and obey') can cause you to stay in a relationship long after the love between you has died or, indeed, prevent you from finding a new partner when your first marriage has come to an end.

A vow of silence

As a spiritual teacher or healer you may at some point have taken a vow of silence that you would not reveal the secrets of your work. It applies if you were a monk or nun in a very strict sect too, or were under threat of persecution for your religious views. The memory of this pledge can result in secretiveness, a reluctance to share knowledge or information or even forgetfulness.

A vow of revenge

Soldiers going into battle often took oaths, or made curses to threaten the enemy and to vow revenge if they were worsted. People who have high blood pressure or a lot of suppressed rage within them may be showing the influence of a previous vow of revenge.

A vow of commitment

If ever you make a heartfelt pledge it remains with you, whether it is in this lifetime or another. The commitment may be to your family ('I will never leave you'), to a cause or to a value (such as justice) or even to a place. It can explain why certain people cling on to life unnecessarily, or reincarnate again and again to fight for something dear to them, or are drawn to a particular location.

KARMIC WOUNDS

I have mentioned earlier that a traumatic situation in a previous incarnation can leave a negative karmic imprint on your soul, and that part of your mission in this life will be to heal it in order to rebalance the light of your soul for your spiritual expansion. It can happen sometimes that, when the incident has a physical aspect, the memory of the wounding, torture or death, for example, can manifest itself in your body as a reminder to you of something to be addressed and healed. If you were strangled you may have a recurring sore throat (and this can also indicate a reluctance to speak your truth); if you died through a spear in your heart, you may have heartburn or indigestion; if you had an arrow in your back, you may have aches and pains or a weakness in that area; if you died in childbirth, you may have gynaecological problems.

I suggest you consider, briefly, your state of health. Do you have a part of your body that is a little weak or vulnerable and you don't know why? If so, it may indicate a karmic wound asking for healing and it may well be linked to an emotional scar which also needs to be addressed.

Certain healers specialise in the removal of karmic vows, wounds and memories, and if your life is being significantly affected by some aspect of karma, then I recommend you consult one. Please see the resources section for more information.

RESPECTING THE KARMA OF OTHERS (THE LAW OF NON-INTERVENTION)

You are among many evolved souls who have come into life at this time to clear your negative karmic balance sheet and advance your spiritual journey. Only you can do this for yourself, even if other people such as family members have a part to play in the scenario. Sometimes, of course, you may wish to ask for help from a professional or someone you trust but, in the end, even with the involvement of others, it is you through your intent and actions who will do the work. Nobody else can do it for you.

It is one of the great spiritual rules that no one should interfere with your karmic mission just as you must not interfere or try to change the karma of someone else. It is easily done, usually through over-enthusiasm and lack of understanding.

Joanna's karmic lesson was to learn about letting go of control. She was following a spiritual path with determination but because she had a strong, dominating mind she had decided her life must be a certain way. She had expectations and spent much of her time analysing herself and her actions, grasping every spiritual straw that she believed would bring her the bliss she craved. She controlled every aspect of her life, including her husband, in order to achieve her dreams.

A friend of hers, also very strong-minded, saw what she was doing. Initially she tried to talk to her about her addiction to control, hoping that bringing it to Joanna's attention would be enough to help her see herself in a different way. This was fine, for her friend was giving Joanna the choice of listening to her words or not and so there was no interference. Unfortunately, the friend did not leave it at that, but pushed and pushed Joanna to change her attitude to the extent that she was trying to control her totally and change her way of living and working: she was then interfering with Joanna's karma. Her intention was good, but it had the result of damaging their friendship and interfering with Joanna's freedom to choose.

So, if you find yourself pushing someone to do something, trying to achieve for someone else what you believe to be right – in your opinion – you may wish to reflect as to if and how far you are preventing that person from following their path in the way they choose. Even a child or someone with mental difficulties will know, innately at the level of their soul, how to heal their karma for themselves, when the time is right and in the way that is appropriate. For ones such as these, guide and teach lovingly and gently, about how to live safely, wisely and happily, but give them also choice and freedom to be who they are as far as you can and as far as is appropriate for their circumstances.

In general, then, give advice by all means, if it is requested, but recognise when advice becomes interference. The wise course is to listen, to give a view if asked, to observe lovingly what that person does, and without judgement, in the knowledge that their decision and mistakes are all for their learning. Your intervention, if it is unwarranted, can inhibit or delay their mission for this lifetime, which would be a great pity.

Exercise 3: Release obsolete karmic vows

Prepare for meditation in the normal way.

State clearly your intention to release old vows or promises that no longer serve you, if it be for the highest good.

Close your eyes, take three deep breaths and go within.

The exercise

- Ask to be taken to a place of significance for you. It may be one you know or one which is foreign to you. Observe where you find yourself, how you feel about it and if you recognise it.

- Ask your two Guardian Angels to join you and to stand alongside you. (See Chapter Seven for more information on your Guardian Angels.)

- Make the following affirmation, adjusting the wording to be comfortable for you. It is very important that you *believe* your affirmation and trust that it will work.

In the name of God, I hereby claim freedom from the influence and power of any and every pledge, oath, vow, curse or other commitment that I have taken upon myself or which has been imposed upon me at any time in any lifetime including the present, which no longer serves me and is not for the highest good.

- Repeat this affirmation twice more, so that you say it three times altogether. End saying, '*So be it.*'

- Wait to see if anything occurs. It is possible you will feel a divine presence. Your angels may make a ritual symbol or movement. You may hear words. Other people may join you. There may be a ceremony. Watch, feel and react as you are guided.

- Give thanks for the release and to your helpers, leave the place and return to your everyday world. Make notes in your spiritual journal if you wish.

- You may feel a little spacey or tired, so ensure you close your chakras and put protection around yourself before going out and about again.

Chapter Three

Life, Death and Reincarnation

Before I consider what living, dying and being reborn means for you, in spiritual terms, it may be helpful to remind you that everything that happens to you is a miniature reflection of what happens to planet Earth, and that your life and actions have a direct influence upon Earth just as Earth has a direct influence upon you. The two are inextricably linked and your spiritual progress through life and death, as a part of humanity, parallels Earth's spiritual progress. Part of your purpose for being born is to help the planet, if you choose, as well as clearing karma and expanding the light of your soul. The planet also wishes to clear karma and expand the soul and you have a role in this.

Let me explain.

Earth herself is on a spiritual journey just as you are. She has a heart, a soul and a personality; she lives and breathes. It is her intention to expand spiritually, just as it is yours whether you know it consciously or not. Unfortunately humanity has not helped in this regard. In his book *The Revenge of Gaia* Professor James Lovelock describes very well the relationship that exists between Earth and humanity, and how through our carelessness and selfishness we have destabilised the delicate balance that has underpinned the health of our planet since it was born, leading to climate change and potential natural disasters.

These events are an outward manifestation of her wounded soul. After hundreds if not thousands of years of abuse, there is much karma to heal between us and the planet which sustains us and gives us life.

WHY CHOOSE A LIFE ON EARTH?

I have explained earlier that it is what you choose to do and how you choose to be that determines how fast your spiritual consciousness expands and your soul evolves. This opportunity to choose, to experience, to learn and to heal karma is only available on Earth. On all the other planets in our solar system progress up the evolutionary ladder can be very slow and so this planet is a very popular destination for souls intent on spiritual growth. The opportunities for learning and spiritual advancement are tremendous.

Also, Earth is in a major period of transition, moving from the Piscean to the Aquarian Age, from one great cycle of time to another. When the transition is complete, which will be soon, a philosophy of profound spirituality will prevail. So, those souls which are awake and able to reincarnate into a physical body at this time and who are alive on Earth now count themselves doubly fortunate to be here, to be part of the acceleration that is occurring for the planet's soul journey and to assist the birth of the new spiritual era.

Let's look in detail now at how reincarnation on Earth applies to you and your soul journey.

REINCARNATION

At some point before you were born it was decided that you would have a life, probably not your first one, on Earth. In other words you would reincarnate. Reincarnation is the rebirth of a soul in a new body and the purpose of reincarnation is to assist the soul to heal, experience, learn and grow – essentially to become more filled with light as a result of your actions, thoughts, intentions and behaviour.

In order to make your choices of conduct freely, without influence or bias, you are not allowed to have any memory when you incarnate. Instead, you have to come to Earth with a veil over the memory of all that has gone before. So, you remember nothing of your past lives, your soul's purpose or your spiritual heritage – all you have is the world you are born into and what you make of it. This explains the pain of being born, because you are leaving the familiarity and security of life as soul and spirit in the non-physical realms followed by a brief period in the warmth and darkness of the womb, only to be pushed or pulled out into the unknown. Often the first thing a baby experiences is physical pain, bright lights, instruments and noise – a terrifying introduction to the world it sought so eagerly to join and it cannot remember why it is here.

The Akashic Records

The pre-planning for a life as a human on Earth is detailed and complex, and being stripped of your memory is one of the final acts in the many preparations for your new incarnation. When it was determined, thousands of years ago while you were a young soul, that you would have a cycle of existence as a human being on Earth, a plan, a template was drawn up which charted every life you might possibly have. The purpose of the Great Plan was so that you could learn all about being human in order to do your service to God and for your soul to grow. This blueprint is part of the Akashic Records. The word 'Akashic' comes from the Sanskrit word for ether, space or spirit.

The Records register everything you (or anyone) have ever done in any lifetime and in between lifetimes; they are the history of you and your spiritual journey, past, present and what is to come, and they are constantly being updated as that journey progresses.

So, if one lifetime has not gone quite according to plan because of the way you have chosen to live it, then the original template for your spiritual journey will be adjusted to ensure the experiences you missed, for example, are learnt next time.

Certain angelic energies (known technically as the 'Lords of Karma') are the keepers of the Akashic Records. It is they, in consultation with you and the spiritual helpers who guide your soul journey, who decide the concept and details of each new incarnation, or rebirth, to bring your next lifetime into perfect manifestation. These spiritual helpers are described in Chapter Seven.

The criteria for rebirth

A number of factors are considered when deciding the new life you will have as a human:

1. Your past life history

Part of the purpose for being 'in body' is to learn what it is to be human, and so the karmic angelic beings will review what lessons you have learnt already from other past life experiences and assess what remains to be done. It may be that in your last life on Earth you were learning about money. If you failed to learn what was intended in that lifetime then it may be that you will be required to return to be taught the same lessons again, or to have new lessons on the same subject. Alternatively, it may be that you have learnt all there is to know and can move on to another subject.

2. Your karma

I examined the subject of karma in detail in the last chapter, but not in the context of the Lords of Karma. These karmic angels are like impartial judges: through the Akashic Records they review the balance of karma which is upon your soul to identify what you have achieved already that is 'good' karma, or light, and what is more negative and needs to be cleared in the next lifetime. If you have abused power for your own ends in a lifetime or a series of lifetimes, and it has been far more than was intended for your learning, thus creating negative karma, then the Lords of Karma may arrange for you to have another life of power so that you can learn to use it wisely and altruistically, to clear the burden upon your soul.

3. Your path to higher evolution

As you become more and more evolved as a soul, at a certain point you will decide what area of spiritual specialisation you will follow when your lifetimes on Earth are complete. When you reach this stage, your final lives in body will be chosen in order to give you the opportunity, through your work or talents, to learn about and practise that path.

Your choices for spiritual specialisation and what this means are considered in the next chapter.

4. Your astrological considerations

When the purpose and overall concept of your new incarnation is decided, the timing of your conception and birth are planned carefully to ensure that you are born into the most appropriate astrological configuration for you in that new life. It is important that the planets and stars influencing you are those that will help your soul to evolve as much as possible and will fulfil the intention for that lifetime. It may mean that your arrival on Earth is delayed until the best planetary arrangement is available.

5. Cosmic influences

Part of the planning process by the Lords of Karma and their angelic assistants is to ensure that each new lifetime enables you to have the appropriate cosmic influences to turn what is a negative frailty in you into a strength and to enhance all that is positive in you – you could say to turn your negative specks of soul-dust into light and to help the light of your soul shine brighter. These cosmic influences impact upon your karma and your soul and are an important part of the lessons you are here to learn for your spiritual expansion.

They are known, technically, as 'the Rays' and they are explained and discussed in detail in Chapter Six.

6. Your evolutionary level

Whatever your evolutionary level, your new life will be designed to give you the background and opportunities to help you move forward to the next stage of your journey with as little difficulty as possible. If you are a soul that is working on lessons to do with physical self-control, for example, or the emotions, your new life will be designed in order to give you as many opportunities to learn about restraint, balance and equanimity. If you are an old soul which is highly evolved because of the degree and speed of your spiritual learning and experience, and which is incarnating to expand into even higher dimensions, you will choose to have a life where you can demonstrate your unconditional love for and wish to help the planet, mankind and beyond.

7. Your environmental needs

The practicalities about life on Earth are meticulously chosen, too, to ensure you have everything you need to achieve your purpose in this new lifetime of yours. This includes the culture you are born into, the geographical location, the colour of your skin, your religion, your class of society, your siblings, if any, your talents, your academic ability, how you look, your state of health and your personality.

Your parents, too, are carefully selected, to give you the genes and biological make-up you need as well as your upbringing, and frequently to clear old karmic residues between you and other family members that may have been carried forward from previous lives. It is often the case that a family group, also family friends and even pets, has been together many times before and your mother may have been your father or brother or child or colleague in the past. Your new life and everything in it is designed carefully to assist you as much as possible. It is up to you what you do with it.

The cycles of reincarnation

So, as a soul learning Earth lessons, you have one complete cycle of many births and rebirths on Earth. The cycle ends when you have achieved a certain level of spiritual learning and development and can be released from the need to reincarnate. Within that one round there are other cycles to assist your growth, experience and knowledge.

I have told you before that you come to Earth school to learn everything there is to know about being human and you may learn a particular lesson about, for example, what love means, over several lifetimes, as long as it takes for you to experience it from all angles. When you understand how to give and receive love wisely, what it means, the negatives and positives about it, you are released from that particular cycle of learning to move onto another cycle of lives for a different lesson.

I mentioned earlier and it bears repeating that, because you have no memory of what has gone before, nor of your spiritual roots, some people who are learning about, for example, integrity and its antithesis corruption get caught up in the material world of dishonesty and greed rather like an addict fixated by a need for drugs. They have to reincarnate again and again in an ever-extending cycle to try to cure their addiction to money and power, but sometimes find it impossible to move on. They are in a downward spiral and in each new lifetime the experience chosen for them is increasingly extreme to try to jolt them out of their habit.

So, while having a life on Earth is the most wonderful chance for your soul to evolve, it also carries with it the danger of getting caught up in the world of matter to such a degree that you never wake up to the reality of who you are as an innate spiritual being.

Lifetime after lifetime can perpetuate the myth of separation from the divine so much that it becomes ingrained and all you have is the illusion that all that exists is the material world which centres upon you and your needs instead of the knowledge that you are, first and foremost, soul and spirit in a human body, part of the great cosmic totality. Society's growing focus, worldwide, on technology and control over the material and natural world is evidence of this trend.

It takes great courage, therefore, to choose to be in body. However, every soul makes it in the end, though it takes some longer than others. This is why, when you see someone or a group of people behaving in a way that seems anti-social, cruel, heartless or misguided, remember that they are learning, struggling to move forward in their own way; do not judge them but rather have compassion for them as souls who may have lost their way.

Reincarnation and animals

Animals have souls too. A herd of cows or a flock of sheep will have a group soul, but domesticated animals can be very wise with their own unique soul, and they reincarnate as we do. Certain animals, fish and birds which are very evolved are, now, at the level where they are able to reincarnate as humans and to begin the long cycle of human learning and experience.

Just as we often have strong soul links with people in our lives, such as family members or certain work colleagues, so those pets which join us, sadly, for just a few years may well have been with us before as animal companions in lifetime after lifetime. So, your cat may have been a hunting dog or a favourite horse of yours, even a parrot. These animals are part of your spiritual team and they return time after time to be in service to us like faithful retainers, and it is our responsibility to care for them and value them as we would a loyal servant.

These special creatures appear in our lives for a purpose and at a specific time. Although their appearance may be different from the last time they were with you, you may recognise something familiar about their personality and you may sense a bond immediately as you look in their eyes. Look closely when a new pet comes into your life, and you will know.

LIFE

Life is spirit, life is God, God is life and because of this your life can never die. When you are in a body, as you are now, your life force is both within the costume that is your body for this lifetime and is also connected to the world of spirit beyond through your soul and spirit. You assume a body-costume which is perfectly chosen for the lessons of a particular lifetime, and when you have completed that life you abandon the costume, discard the body and your life continues in the non-physical realms until you are ready to put on another, different costume over your life force.

Everything that exists contains a life force, even the chair you are sitting in and the cup by your hand. Every thing is connected to Spirit, every thing has a life and an energy of its own and it is important, if you can, to remember this when you are in your everyday life. When a drawer sticks, instead of trying to force it open be gentle with it as if it were a child; when you are washing up, be aware of and focused upon each piece of china or cutlery which serves you so well. If you honour all that is around you, whether it is a plant in your garden, your cat or your washing machine, it will co-operate with you; being violent, angry or uncaring will bring negativity back to you like a boomerang.

Every thing that is yours, that you use, has a part of your life energy too. This is why so many people like to use the same cup for their morning coffee or to sit in the same place while watching television. The cup and the seat, everything you use regularly, have your energy embedded in them as well as what they bring in their own right.

Why is life so painful?

You may sometimes wonder why it seems so hard to find peace of mind and heart, instead having to deal with a life of constant worry and struggle. Remember, every difficulty, indeed every situation, presents itself as an opportunity to learn and grow. You have chosen to be here to progress and in Earth school you have to take the occasional test and repeat it until you pass. If there is a pattern in your life which seems to have been there for ever, such as falling out with people regularly, then this is one of your main lessons for this lifetime, and by looking at it and recognising it for what it is you can do something about it.

For some people life can be particularly difficult and you may know one or two individuals who have had to undergo great sorrow and challenge, far more than seems fair. Some brave souls, when their new life was being planned with the Lords of Karma, are so keen to get as much as possible out of their time on Earth that they ask to experience their hardest lessons in the course of the one incarnation, rather than spreading them over several lifetimes. It may involve loss of loved ones, financial hardship, serious ill-health and great disappointments or disaster. If you have known anyone in this sort of a situation, you may have noticed how well able, so often, they are to cope with all that has assailed them, have admired their courage and been amazed at their resilience.

On the other hand, not every lifetime is one of intense learning, and you will have lifetimes which are peaceful and uneventful as well as incarnations that are momentous. This often occurs if you have had a particularly traumatic previous life: because the trauma may impact your soul for a long time after the event that caused it, often it will be arranged for you to have a subsequent life, or lifetimes, of healing and recuperation to help your soul recover.

You will also have a place somewhere, a region or country, which is special to you and to which you feel a particular affinity and which is your sanctuary and place of healing.

A client of mine, Caroline, had a cycle of lives over a 1,200 year period learning about persecution and finally ended that cycle when she was massacred as a Cathar Priest at Béziers. She had experienced witchunts as the witch and the judge, she had lit the fires, been the jailor, the inquisitor, the wife and child of the persecuted and the persecutor, and finally, for many lifetimes, she was the victim. There was nothing she did not know about persecution from every angle, and so she was, at last, able to cease that particular aspect of learning about being human.

When she reincarnated again she was given a tranquil and happy life in Wales as a loving mother and respected member of her community, which literally was balm to her soul and which enabled her, in her next lifetime, to start a new cycle of lessons, this time to do with the wise use of power.

In her case, whenever she needed a lifetime of recovery, she always returned to Wales which for her was and is her sanctuary.

Spirituality in early life

A child's experience of life on Earth begins before it is born. While it is in its mother's womb it can sense what is occurring beyond, particularly through the feelings and emotions of the mother herself to which the baby is very sensitive. When the mother is calm and relaxed it will help her child and if she communicates with the child lovingly, even without words, her baby will sense it and be comforted. Similarly, if the mother is troubled, anxious or fearful, her baby will feel it also. Some babies, often those who are old souls, because of their love for their parent take upon themselves her sadness or negativity in order to help her.

Deirdre, one of the most compassionate people I know, was conceived when her mother was grieving for the loss of her firstborn in a terrible accident. Because of her love for her mother she chose, even in the womb, to take that grief upon herself which meant that, when she was born, she came into the world already burdened with a weight of negativity which was not actually hers.

For many years she cheerfully and uncomplainingly continued to try to protect her mother, and it was only when she sought help to identify why she could not overcome her innate sadness and loneliness that she discovered what, as a loving soul, she had done. She recognised that it was appropriate for the memories and emotions which were not hers to be released and, through healing, and her own self-awareness and spiritual practice, she was able to move forward and, at last, to be herself. She is now married with children and very happy.

Many 'experts' believe that babies have short-term memories, but it is my belief that this is not so. Babies have souls and so what the baby experiences is registered on its soul just as what an adult thinks or does has a soul impact. From my work with one or two people using past life regression I have encountered situations where they have demonstrated quite clearly accurate recollections of people and places that they only came across in the first few months of their life.

Spirituality in childhood

For some advanced souls the veil of spiritual oblivion does not come down immediately they come into incarnation. It varies from person, but a child can, exceptionally, be a few years old before he or she forgets all that has gone before. As I will explain in Chapter Seven, everyone who is in body has a spiritual team of helpers standing by to assist and support the purpose of their incarnation – if their soul is awake. Some sensitive children can see and communicate with one or more of these helpers, or imaginary friends, until something happens to stop it or it is time for the mantle of forgetfulness to come down.

Most young children totally trust their parents, their mother in particular, and believe everything they say is correct. If their mother says or does something to destroy that child's belief in his or her own experience or sense of self, it can cause the spiritual connection they still have to cease, sometimes resulting in serious emotional damage to the child. There must be no judgement or blame if this occurs. A child in this situation will be learning about separation and trust, and the harder the lesson the greater the need. There may even be some karmic issues between mother and child being resolved. Opportunities to study and pass the Earth school tests are always being given.

Spirituality in later life

When the veil of oblivion comes upon you, whenever it is, you forget everything except what you have experienced in your new life so far. Any memories of your spiritual helpers will be like an imaginary dream, if they last at all.

Your life, thereafter, is one of living and being in your carefully chosen body and personality, learning and growing, taking your tests when you are ready and enabling your soul to evolve through what you have experienced and done. If you have not taken up the opportunities that were intended for you by the time you come to leave this incarnation, the Lords of Karma will determine what would serve you best for your next lifetime on Earth and when it should be, and the planning process for reincarnation will begin again. In such cases you are likely to come back very rapidly in order to make up for lost time.

More evolved souls may spend longer in the non-physical realms, sometimes (in our terms) for hundreds of years, being taught and prepared for what lies ahead on their spiritual journey, but always it will be the Lords of Karma and their angelic associates who will decide, with you, how and when your next life will be.

Lost souls

There is such a thing as a lost soul, but it is most unusual. Some souls become so trapped in a cycle of depravity they cannot escape, nor do they want to. They have become addicted to that which serves their soul least, such as an insatiable and totally self-centred hunger for power, money or sexual depravity.

If a soul, during a lifetime, cannot say or do one kind word or deed in the whole of that lifetime then it is likely that it has chosen to separate totally from Spirit, and it cannot return to the godhead. Instead, it lingers in a lower dimension with other lost souls. It is very terrible when this happens, but also very rare. I have never come across it. However depraved the entity, there is always the opportunity for it to learn and to begin its ascent up the spiritual ladder once again, to be welcomed home with love and honour.

DEATH

As part of the cycle of death and rebirth, everything that is in existence dies, is reborn and dies and is reborn again. It happens to you, to our animals, to our houses (yes, this sounds strange, but when buildings crumble the matter they consist of returns to the earth and that earth one day regenerates as plant life, a rock or even material to be used for another construction) and to the trees, to give just a few examples. Our planet was born once and will die many years from now, and then will be reborn but with a different appearance and the same process will occur to our solar system and all the stars and planets within it. Even when you are in incarnation, you experience small deaths and rebirths as you evolve and leave a part of yourself in your past, whether it is a bad habit or reaching a particular transition point in your Earth lessons. Your hair and skin and nails die and regenerate all the time.

When you go to sleep you experience a form of dying. You become unconscious before you begin to dream, just as you do in the early stages of death, and because your soul is no longer trapped in your body it has freedom to fly to wherever it wishes to go in the higher realms, returning as you begin to wake up like a mini-rebirth. When you sleep the life force does not leave you, but when you die it does.

So, death is always around us, a necessary part of the natural rhythm of spiritual life and to be celebrated as marking achievement and opportunity, the end of one phase and the beginning of another. For you as a human being, death means the return home to the world of Spirit, a release from the dark world of matter and oblivion. It is inevitable, unavoidable and for many people a terrifying thought. In fact, it is very wonderful.

How and when you die

Part of the planning process for each of your incarnations is not just when you will be born (as well as all the other criteria for a new life discussed above) but also when and how you will die. So, there is nothing random about how or when your body dies, but the manner and timing of your going may depend on a number of reasons:

A painful death

- This can be an opportunity for you and your friends and relatives to learn about suffering.

- This can help to heal rifts and wounds between family members.

- This can strengthen you whether you are the patient or the carer through having to deal with the experience.

- This can be because it is what you think you deserve, a form of self-punishment if you have issues to do with self-worth.

- This can even be brought about by focused or obsessive fear or thinking, again demonstrating the power of thought that I discussed in Chapter One. A dear friend of mine talked to me very recently about the death of her mother from bowel and liver cancer, which was exactly what killed her father years before. She believed that her mother missed him so much she subconsciously induced the same exit for herself, and indeed this can happen.

Please remember that you can manifest what you think about, wish for or fear through the power of your thoughts. If you worry obsessively that you will have a painful death, it is possible that that is what you will create for yourself, but if you are philosophical and accepting about it, it will assist the likelihood of your death being easy.

A lingering death
Sometimes a loved one can find it hard to leave their body and move on. It can be because of their resistance or stubbornness, or it can be the result of the longing of grieving relatives desperate for them to stay. It is natural to hope that there will be a recovery or that you will have a little more time together, but praying for the outcome *you* want is not always in the best interests of the one who is preparing to leave, because the strength of your emotions and wishes can hold them back when they are ready to go.

In such a case it is best to pray for what is best for *them*, and to send them as much love as possible. I will look at how you can help a loved one through the dying process shortly.

Unfinished business
Someone who is dying may linger through his fear of the unknown, the taboo of death, or it may be there is some

unfinished business with a family member, something that he or she intended to clear in that lifetime but which remains outstanding. If you believe this is the case with someone you know, it can help to encourage them to talk about it. If your own relationship has been difficult with your mother or father, then to express, lovingly and kindly, what you have been unable to say for so long can help to clear the air. Even if the person who is dying is unconscious, when you speak to them they will hear you and feel your love.

If you find it impossible to speak about it directly, then you may write to them – but you will not post the letter! – your soul speaking to their soul, saying what you feel, perhaps expressing forgiveness or asking for it and also telling them that they are free to leave their body whenever they wish, that you will not hold them back from going home.

When you have said what you wish in your letter, burn it and ask Spirit to take it to your relative or friend. This will happen and it can have remarkable results.

A sense of commitment or duty

Sometimes a dying parent who has always worried about the well-being of their child frets about what will happen to them after they are gone, whatever age their child is, and this also can cause them to linger longer than necessary. Writing a letter to reassure them you will be fine or telling them this will help you both: their soul will know what you have said and the loving intention behind it.

Exit points

Arrangements don't always go to plan and sometimes a soul comes into body to find there is something about the new life experience which is not what was intended and which may cause the mission to go awry. It may be, for example, that the mother chosen for you does not have all the qualities that were anticipated to help your learning or the plan proves to be over-ambitious.

So that a lifetime is not wasted, exit points are built into the plan at various stages of your life so that your soul can leave the body it has chosen sooner than intended originally if it wishes. If you are given permission to go (you cannot leave unilaterally) you will return home and consult with the Lords of Karma who will decide what happens next and when and how you will return to Earth again. If you wish to leave earlier than intended there is no judgement – you have done nothing wrong.

Any premature or unexpected death is always painful, and it can be hard, I know, to see the bigger picture amidst the grief and emotional upheaval. I, perhaps like you, have had my own loss relating to a child, and know how terrible that can be. One of my fundamental beliefs is that everything happens for a reason, to teach us or show us something, and this applies to losing what may be most dear to us. I realise it may be hard to understand, but when there is a cot death, when a child or adult dies in an accident, if a baby gets meningitis, if someone dies younger than would normally be expected, often it is the soul deciding to take an early exit point that has been made available to it. If so, it will be for a reason, even if we do not know what it is. If you have a near-miss in a car accident but survive, a serious illness but pull through, they are times when you have the opportunity to leave, they are exit points, but you have decided after all to stay on Earth. Near death experiences are exit points also.[1]

You may have as many as seven optional exit points at fixed points during a lifetime, any of which or none of which you may choose, through the soul, to ask to use.

Suicide

Some people see suicide as a sin or a sign of weakness, but it is neither. It takes a great deal of courage to kill yourself deliberately (I am not speaking of an accidental death such as an unintended drugs overdose) and it is one of the hardest things you can do. The person aiming consciously to end his or her life is unlikely, consciously, to know the spiritual truth about life and death and so they will be feeling great fear as well as the human despair underlying the deed.

Mariella came to me because her brother had taken his life in a particularly painful way and she wanted to know why it had happened and how he was. When we explored it we discovered that hundreds of years ago he had been a warlord in Mongolia who had very brutally maimed and killed many people, incurring much negative karma upon his soul. At the time of his dying in that lifetime he was filled with guilt for what he had done and resolved in future to ensure others always controlled his actions so that never again could he misuse his power.

In this lifetime, a quiet obedient boy, abused and bullied at school and in the Army where he ended up, he was indeed totally controlled all his life – until he ended his life on Earth. His soul lesson was to break the karma in order to be free to be himself and the most effective way to do this was for him to take control of his body and his life once again in a demonstrably violent act. Not only did this free his soul, but the shock of the event and the abuse that apparently drove him to it taught valuable and necessary lessons for the Army and his family.

He was and is fine, by the way, preparing for his next life, which will be magnificent.

Because there are other ways of leaving an incarnation by using the exit points available, suicide often but not always is a deliberately determined part of the plan for that lifetime. There may be karmic implications both for the individual and those around him or her which can only be resolved through intentional self-killing, or it can be an act of great love carried out in order to help the growth and learning of those who are left behind, although the personality is unlikely to know this at the time. Any act, however large or small, has a purpose and repercussions at many levels.

Murder

Like suicide, murder can occur as part of the cycle of learning about being human and clearing karma. In human terms it is very terrible and heart-rending for the people who find themselves directly or indirectly affected by the taking of a life. However much our spiritual understanding tells us that there may be deeper reasons for the situation that we are observing, our heart feels that an individual and the sanctity of their life has been dishonoured.

It is hard to remember that you and I almost certainly will have experienced brutal death in some way during our cycle of many lifetimes as part of our learning about being human, but this is so. Fortunately, for most of us our learning about the different aspects of murder has taken place hundreds or thousands of years ago when life was cheap and short and the experience is done and not to be repeated.

Trapped in past memory

Sometimes quite a period of time, in human terms, (time in the non-physical world is very different from linear time as we know it: it is based on the present, and thousands of human years pass in seconds in the spirit world) elapses between one incarnation and the next. It doesn't happen very often, but a soul which was last in body in, say, the Dark Ages, may reincarnate into our present society and culture with an ingrained memory of the norms of the life he had last, and it can be very difficult for him or her to see that those norms may be inappropriate for the society they are living in now.

It is usual that your childhood experiences teach you what is acceptable behaviour for your new life, but very occasionally the previous beliefs are very strong and difficult to replace. For example, a paedophile may have had his last life in Victorian England where child abuse was, compared to now, accepted behaviour in some circles. A present-day murderer of prostitutes may have been a burner of witches last time round. The paedophile and the persecutor may therefore genuinely not understand why their behaviour is considered to be unacceptable. It does not, of course, excuse their conduct, but demonstrates how hard the Earth learning can be for some people.

A relative of a friend of mine was promiscuous throughout his adult life and felt mystified as to why his wife first of all could not accept his conduct as natural and then refused to agree to his plan that she and his latest mistress should live together happily in a *ménage à trois*, along with their children.

In this case, his sense of morality came from a different era and he had become locked into a cycle of sexual selfishness. Part of his learning was to move on from there and to learn about integrity in relationships and about honouring his wife after many lifetimes of abusing her.

It was a lesson he was unable to learn. He married five times, each relationship foundering because of his many affairs, and when he died aged 58 he had no regrets for the pain he had caused so many people, including his children. His affection for his first wife, however, endured until the end, and I am sure they will have a lifetime together again in order to clear the karma that is outstanding still between them.

THE GREAT TABOO

It is at this point in our discussion about death that you may start to feel a little uncomfortable. I am going to get personal. I encourage you to read on because what I have to say is important and enlightening.

Death, as has been said elsewhere, is the great certainty of life, even more than taxes. It comes to us all, whatever our background or status, and the only difference between us is the reason for and manner and timing of our going. In some parts of the world death is part of the way of life and celebrated for where it takes you and it used to be the same for us: thousands of years ago our pagan rituals celebrated death just as they embraced nature and existence too.

Now, particularly in the Western world, death is a taboo subject. Most people do not want to think about their own death or the death of loved ones and some individuals are reluctant even to make a will because the act of so doing relates to their demise. Very few of us think about our funerals and talk about what we would like to have as a send-off. Even fewer talk to our families about how we would like our dying to be – and hardly anyone thinks about or wants to know what actually happens when we die.

Thinking about these aspects of death is a little like checking the bank statement you have been dreading opening. By putting it off for weeks, the fear of what you may find gets bigger every time you think about it, which is probably every day. When you pluck up the courage to open the envelope and look you may not like what you see or you may be pleasantly surprised, but either way you will know what the position is and can then decide what to do about it. It is the not knowing and the imaginings of the what-ifs which are the worst.

So it is with death. Despite the not looking, pretending it will never happen or at least not for a long time, you know deep within you that something 'unpleasant' lies ahead that is inevitable – but very probably you have little idea, as with your unopened bank statement, about the reality of what is in that particular end-of-life envelope.

That is what this section is all about. I want to open the envelope of death and explain to you, quite simply, how you can make practical and spiritual preparations for someone's death, what happens when you die and where you go afterwards, so that you can see that it is a wonderful, natural and straightforward process. You may not be quite ready to welcome death as you would Christmas, but I hope some greater understanding of this important subject will help you be ready for when your own time comes and also help you when loved ones are going through their own death process.

Preparation and ritual in the death process

In ancient Egypt death was taken very seriously because it marked the beginning of the journey into the afterlife. It was considered crucial that the individual was prepared psychologically and physically before death and that certain rituals were performed during and after death to assist the journey of the soul. The more aristocratic the dying person, the more elaborate was the ritual, which could last for days. It was considered a privilege to assist the dying to make their transition and it was a time of joy, ceremony, singing and chanting.

All the major civilisations have had their own ways of marking death, some of them intensely profound. In the Western world now, the process can be distorted by medical interference and logistical prioritisation so that the dying process often is managed by drugs in a noisy environment where the patient is treated as an object not a person. When a body is clinically dead it is removed and dealt with as quickly as possible and rarely is there recognition or understanding by nursing or caring staff, however well-intentioned as many of them are, that the dying process is more than just the apparent death of the body tissue at an apparent point in time.

If you are watching a loved one approaching death there are certain steps you can take to assist them. Let's look at what can be done well ahead of time when they are comparatively well and their departure seems distant, or if there are indications it may not be so far away, perhaps because of health issues becoming apparent.

Beforehand

1. If you feel comfortable, and if they will be receptive, talk to them ahead of time about death, life and rebirth to ease their fears and to let them know that their passing, whenever it is, is a beginning and not an end. One of the reasons so many people fear the thought of dying is because they see it as a time when they leave all they have known and loved to become nothing. There is also the fear of the unknown. It can be very comforting to be told (even if they say they cannot believe it) that they will be reunited with relatives who have passed over before and will do so later and that they will be coming back to Earth.

2. Try to anticipate if there is anything outstanding in every day terms: is there a will? Is it up to date? Do you know where it is? Where are the papers kept? Do you need a key to the house? Who is in charge of the arrangements? Yes, I know this sounds intrusive, but it is possible and indeed a good idea to be up front and to say something along the lines of, 'Now, I hope it is a long time away before we need to do anything about it, but for my peace of mind can I ask you some business questions so that we are both sure everything is taken care of and then we don't have to mention it again.'

3. Encourage your loved one to indicate what sort of a funeral they would like. If you do this while they are comparatively well and death seems some way away it will be easier to talk about it – and then they and you can forget about it until the time comes when it is necessary to do so. Again, it is possible to introduce the subject quite lightly, perhaps by saying

what funeral you yourself would like and asking for their views.

What I am suggesting here is, I know, delicate for all of you who are involved in the situation. You may yourself be feeling a little emotional and you may not wish to talk about issues to do with finality for their sake as well as yours. However, I promise you that if you can gently raise the matters suggested when you feel the time is right, it will be of tremendous benefit. Often, you know, just to ask one question will provide the opportunity to clarify all you need to know for when the time comes. It will bring you closer together and can be reassuring to all of you who are involved.

When death approaches

1. Try to ascertain if the one who is leaving wishes to die at home or if they prefer to be in a clinic or hospital. The majority of people would prefer to spend their final days in the place they have known and loved but, sadly, this is usually denied them because of the requirements of the medical or care systems we have in the Western world. In some countries it is possible to obtain specialist charitable nursing care to enable patients to die with dignity at home, a wonderful but little-known service.

2. When you and your friend or relative know that death is not very far away, ask your loved one if there is anything they want to be arranged for them for when their time of death comes. Is there any music they would like in their room, special flowers, a candle, anyone they would wish to be present – or not?

   Some people, I know, will be so filled with fear they will not wish to acknowledge their death is close at hand and so will refuse to discuss such matters. However, the more you can talk about death and what it means, how wonderful and natural it is and how you want to make it the best possible occasion for them, the easier it will be for you and for them. If you feel you cannot discuss such matters with them, I suggest you follow your own intuition as to what to do and determine how, discreetly, you can introduce anything that may be relaxing and calming.

3. Ask ahead of time the nursing or medical staff to administer only what is necessary by way of drugs for pain relief or medical need as the time of death approaches. The freer of drugs and chemicals we are when we die, the easier and clearer the release into the next world.

4. If he or she is in hospital or a clinic, try to arrange for your loved one to have a private room and maximum privacy.

5. When it is clear that death is not far away, ask the staff or carers to honour the wishes of the dying person and explain what you propose to do to help them, such as putting their favourite flowers in their room, playing gentle music if they would like this, having gentle rather than harsh lighting. Explain how you would wish the dying process, at the time, to be handled, if it is appropriate.

6. At this time there may be much grief and sadness from the family and friends of your loved one and you may be feeling the pain as well, however much you understand the higher beauty of the situation. If you can, explain to them the importance of allowing your loved one to leave the Earth plane when they are ready and not to try to keep them with you longer than they would wish. Encourage them to pray for your loved one's highest good and well-being, not, specifically, their continuing survival in body.

7. If your friend or relative has not expressed a preference, have ready a scented candle or incense sticks for when the need for them comes. The scents will mask any antiseptic and medical smells as well as bringing pleasure to the senses of all involved and the candle flame will be a focus of light. Now is the time to ask for gentle lighting not harsh overhead lights if it can be arranged.

8. Allow the room to be as quiet as possible – if music has been requested, let it be muted – to enable the dying person to focus on his or her process without distraction. It is not always helpful to have a lot of people around, particularly if they are emotional. Animals slip away to die alone if they can, and humans too often choose to die at a time when other people, particularly grieving loved ones, are out of the room momentarily.

9. When the body of your loved one is clinically dead remember that the death process is not complete and there is still a lot going on. Try to maintain the atmosphere of quiet and reverence that you have created. Ask for the body to be allowed to rest where it is for at least a half hour, and when it has to be moved try to arrange for it to go to a place – morgue, undertakers or the equivalent – nearby. Because the etheric body may still be exiting through its chosen chakra for quite some time – I explain this shortly – the less movement and disruption there is to the body the better.

10. Finally, give thanks for the successful transition of your loved one to their next life on a new plane of existence in the knowledge they are close to you still, even if you cannot see them now, and that you will be with them again both in your world now and when you yourself move on.

I know, you have read this guidance and are wondering about it and if you could do it? Is it necessary? Would it make any difference?

I will say this to you and you can judge for yourself. When I was writing this chapter, three clients and friends of mine quite separately called me in the space of two days. All were young women, all had mothers who were dying of cancer. All wanted to know from me what could they do to help their mothers' transition? All were loving daughters who wished to do the best they could, but they did not know what to do. So, I suggested to each of them what I have suggested to you and they followed the advice.

I kept in touch with them while their mothers moved towards their final hours, admiring so much the courage, grace and dignity with which they coped. Afterwards, each one told me how understanding the process and adopting these procedures helped. They also told me how privileged they felt to have been part of and a witness to a time of such importance and that being so very much involved in helping their mothers' passing to the next world helped their grieving process enormously.

It may be that you who are reading these words are facing death soon. I hope so much that they help you to have trust in what lies ahead for you, and to prepare yourself and your friends and relatives to make it as uplifting and beautiful an occasion as it possibly can be.

Let's look now at the dying process itself. This is a factual, technical description of what is, in essence, a wonderful but business-like procedure.

What happens when you die?

1. When your soul knows it is time for your body to die, it begins the process to release you from the world of matter by stimulating your pituitary gland to release a certain hormonal substance into your bloodstream. The 'death hormone', as it is known, and which has been the subject of study by endocrinologists, scientists and others in recent years, affects your heart, precipitating coma or unconsciousness, and initiates the detachment and calm that is so often noticeable among those who are dying.

2. Your attention now is on the higher planes and you are preparing to leave your body. Your consciousness is withdrawing from the world of matter and the preparation for the separation of your etheric body from your physical body is under way.[2] If you are an advanced soul, this inner focus is carried out consciously and deliberately, otherwise it is automatic and may occur while you are physically unconscious.

3. Your etheric body, as it is the vehicle for your soul, begins to leave your physical body through whichever chakra is appropriate for your level of spiritual evolution. If you are an advanced soul you will leave through the crown chakra. If you have lived a loving, well-intentioned and therefore spiritual life you will leave through the heart chakra. For the majority of people their etheric body will exit through the solar plexus chakra because they are not yet spiritually awake.

4. As this process of leaving the physical body begins for you, you will see a very bright tunnel of light which is the Light of God. This light is an important opportunity to expand your spiritual consciousness significantly and in order to achieve this you must merge with that light. If, through fear, you fail to do so, you will have another opportunity to merge with it at a later stage.

5. Besides the light you may see angels, Masters, loved ones and archetypes, such as Merlin or the Divine Mother, and it is at this point, if the soul changes its mind and decides to stay in body after all, that the dying process can cease or possibly be delayed sometimes for weeks while the final outcome is being determined. If you decide to continue, you proceed down the tunnel of light, merge with the light and are welcomed home by those who await you with love and eagerness.

6. When you have left your physical body, because its life force is no longer there to vitalise it the costume of skin and bone and tissue that you have worn throughout your lifetime is technically dead, but, whether it is later destroyed by fire, buried or eaten by fishes it will take form again, for everything is reborn as I discussed earlier in this chapter. Your etheric body eventually dies also, releasing you as a soul to take your place in the dimension which reflects your level of spirituality, as described below.

What happens after death?

1. Review and Healing

When you have passed through the tunnel and merged with the light, the likelihood is that you will return to the astral plane where most souls reside when they are not in body on Earth. The astral plane is in the fourth dimension, just beyond the third-dimensional world of Earth. Because it is a non-physical equivalent of the Earth plane you have just left, it is still connected to the Earth. The three different planes, or dimensions, available to souls in the afterlife are described below.

Whichever dimension you return to, one of the first things that happens is that you will review the life that you have just completed fully and with total clarity, in the context of all your past lives and what was intended to be achieved in this one. It is like an end of term report so that you can see where you have done well and where some improvement is necessary. It is an essential part of the preparation for what you do next and enables you and the Lords of Karma to assess what future lessons are necessary and how best they should be taught, as I mentioned when talking about reincarnation earlier.

Following your review you will go through a form of healing, like a deep sleep, to repair the damage that may have occurred as the result, for example, of a lengthy illness before you died. Remember, at this point you are still in effect a human being but without a physical body and any pain or suffering you have experienced as you left the world of matter will have left its scars.

The healing can take as long as six months, in our terms of time. When it is done if, as is likely, you are living on the astral plane, you can decide how you wish to appear to the other people who are with you there. Many choose to look as they were in their prime in the life they have just left – recognisable to those who know them and at their best. You are likely to have a different appearance in every sojourn on the astral plane, just as you do in each new lifetime on earth.

Babies and young children often choose to continue to grow so that their character and features become established, but may cease to develop when they are in their teens. Remember, whatever appearance you have, you do not have a physical body made of flesh and blood as you did when you were living on Earth, but a body which is light and insubstantial, yet with clearly identifiable 'human' features.

The more spiritually evolved you are, living and working in far distant dimensions, the more you are known by your light, your colour and your sound, and you no longer have any appearance of being human.

2. Meeting loved ones

Unless they have reincarnated already, which would be unusual, you will see your loved ones briefly when you are entering the tunnel of light at the time of your death. They are part of the welcoming party, but you will not see them again until the review and healing are complete. When that is done, it is the time when you can have a joyful reunion with friends and relatives who predeceased you and you can spend as much 'time' as you like with them.[3]

You will still feel a strong attachment with those whom you left behind and may wish to be with them as much as possible, though it may be puzzling at first that they don't seem to see or hear you. Eventually, your need to be with those you love on Earth will lessen as you learn emotional detachment – as you will.

3. Life on the astral plane

Because most people are struggling with control of their body, desires, fears and emotions throughout their life on Earth, after death they will live on the astral plane for some time until they have learnt to forgo the weaknesses that cause them to be in that particular dimension of learning. They will have the opportunity periodically to return to Earth in body to refine who they are but until they have learnt detachment from the world of glamour and illusion they will continue to return to the astral plane. This is why it is so important in this and any lifetime to learn about emotional control, self-discipline, restraint and generosity. Until you do you cannot evolve spiritually.

As you settle in you will feel in many ways as if you are still on Earth, but in heaven on Earth. You can be with those you left behind whenever you wish and you have friends and relatives, even pets, who have died before you around you once again. Whatever you want to have in your new life is available to you and you live that life as you choose.

Life on the astral plane life is often a reflection of how you chose to live on the Earth plane. If you were a drug addict you will hang around with other drug addicts in the sorts of places you frequented before, and drugs will be available to you still if you wish to have them. If you were very house-proud you will create the home of your dreams and spend all your time cleaning it, because it gives you pleasure or because you feel you must. Even though you don't have a physical body, you may nonetheless believe you need to eat and drink because that is what you did before.

My father, who died in 1979, chose to be on a boat sailing round the world, his only companion being a beloved dog. My grandmother, who loved children, chose to live in a large house very like the home she loved in Kent where she could care for her grandchildren and great grandchildren who had died in infancy.

You can create, on the astral plane, any reality you choose, you can go anywhere you want, and because time does not exist it is instantaneous. You decide you would like to go to the beach and find yourself there as soon as you have had the thought.

So, this astral heaven of yours is essentially a self-centred one, based on your wishes and perceived needs for self-gratification. Eventually and inevitably the astral part of you will die as the physical part did and you will move to live on a higher non-physical plane when you have learnt control over your emotions and desires.

4. Life on the mental plane

If you are a more advanced soul you will, depending on your level, go to higher dimensions immediately with no need to reach them via the astral plane. Two other levels are possible beyond the astral: the first is the mental plane which is more cerebral than the astral plane. The heaven you create here will be more thoughtful, less hedonistic than the astral plane, though still with you as the centrepiece, and you will be learning how to be dispassionate and detached and less self-centred.

5. Life on the plane of oneness

The highest level you can go to following an incarnation or between incarnations is Nirvana, the place where God resides. This is only accessible to you when you have cleared all karma and have achieved a level of spiritual greatness. You are an individual still, but concerned with the needs of others and not your own. It is the place of bliss. If you are able to access Nirvana, then you have no need to reincarnate for there is no karma to heal or lessons to learn. However, some souls, through their love for humanity and Earth, choose to return to Earth in physical body for several more lifetimes in order to teach, guide and lead by word, deed and example. Depending on the purpose behind their return, they may reincarnate with full knowledge and memory of their spiritual lineage and mission, or with the mantle of oblivion upon them, like the majority of people.

Exercise 4: Visit your spiritual home between lifetimes

Prepare for meditation in the usual way.

Define and state your intention, which is to go to the plane which is your spiritual home between lifetimes to meet someone dear to you.

Put protection around yourself as suggested in the notes on meditation.

Close your eyes, take three deep breaths and go within.

- See yourself outside a tunnel. It may be a railway tunnel, a large pipe, a tunnel in a cliff face, a place you know or which is imaginary. As you look inside you see a mist or cloud within. Start to walk inside the tunnel if you are ready and willing.

- Move through the mist, you are quite safe. Look ahead and you start to see the mist clearing and light appearing, signalling that the end of the tunnel is in sight.

- As you get closer to the end of the tunnel the light becomes stronger and you may start to see objects, movement, colours beyond, and even to hear sounds.

- Stand at the exit and look through, observe carefully what is there. You are looking at your idea of heaven.

- If you wish, move on and out into this new world. Walk around and explore – it may be familiar or quite new.

- Now, ask for someone close to you to appear. If you trust they will come. It may be a relative or friend who has died, or it may be an angel or Master who is one of your spiritual helpers. Talk with them if you wish. Don't be surprised if you feel a little emotional.

- When you are ready, give thanks to them and return through the tunnel to your everyday reality.

Make notes in your spiritual journal if you wish. Remember to close down your chakras and to put protection around yourself before you return to your everyday world.

Chapter Four

The Soul's Journey

This chapter is about you. It is about your connection to God, how you are part of God and God is part of you, and how this is the essence of your spirituality and the heart of your soul's journey.

Some of the concepts I write about here may seem strange if you have not come across them before, but if you can grasp the principles and purpose underpinning your spiritual destiny, which is what this is all about, then you will be able to understand the beauty and magnificence and the reality of your connection to the totality of all that is. You will realise that you are far, far more than an ordinary human being living out your life as best you can in an everyday world.

You see, your soul is the bridge between you as an individual in this lifetime and God. Its purpose is to journey through many, many lifetimes on behalf of God, reincarnating again and again in order to experience and, from this, to expand spiritually. When the journey of learning and growing on Earth is complete you will be a highly evolved spiritual being of light, ready to return to God, your source, and ready also to start a new cycle of exalted spiritual existence somewhere else, very probably, in the universe.

This is such a fascinating and important subject – the key to understanding your spiritual lineage and destiny. Let's look at all of this in detail, starting at the very beginning.

SO, WHO OR WHAT IS GOD?

The simple answer is that nobody knows, though many, many people claim they do, just as many people claim there is no such thing as God. The nature of God and whether God exists is perhaps the hardest to answer and most controversial question ever. It is the ultimate mystery.

Part of the conundrum about God is, how many Gods are there and where are they? I am not speaking here about the archetypal gods like Apollo and Zeus, but 'our' God. Yes, God is everything and everywhere, influencing and creating everything we know in our world and our universe – but what if there is something even greater beyond that? Suppose there are more universes beyond ours, huge seas of consciousness that are so vast our minds cannot grasp the idea of them? And suppose there is another God, another Source, at the heart of these distant universes?

I believe this is so, that the God who guides your life and who pervades your known world is overshadowed by another even greater divine energy. It is a hypothesis which has been hinted at by the great theosophists and philosophers before them. I leave it to you to ponder this idea and I appreciate it may be unbelievable or incomprehensible. See how it feels for you. For your purposes in reading this book it is not necessary to have an opinion either way, though I may hint at the concept of something greater than 'our' God from time to time. Generally speaking, when I refer to God I will be referring to the God you know, the God who guides your life and governs the solar system and what lies beyond.

Now I will explain how God made you what you are, according to my own understandings and beliefs.

IN THE BEGINNING . . .

God created light, the solar system, planet Earth, life, and it could be said that it was God's will that enabled it to happen. God wished it to be and it was. There was nothing random about it. Indeed, underpinning Creation there is an amazing cosmic order and organisation which is the great Plan of God and which you are a part of now and will be for ever.

Part of God's Plan is to expand, and it may be helpful to see all space as a great expanse of spiritual consciousness, of Light, which is constantly increasing in accordance with the Plan. The Light of spiritual consciousness, God's Light, is assisted in its expansion by souls like you who, through your experiences and choices, are able to grow your own light which then becomes part of the totality which is God. And so God is able to grow with your help.

Let me explain how you become involved in all of this. Long before you existed, it began with . . .

THE MONAD

To achieve God's aim of expanding, it was decided to send out divine 'sparks' of God to every place in the universe: part of God, you could say, became active in order to learn and grow and expand the Light. These divine sparks are known as Monads – 'the One', 'the First'. They are the source of everything, and the ultimate unit, or constituent, of being.

Each Monad comes from God and therefore is pure spirit, perfection. Because it is a part of God it cannot be anything but perfect and always will be. Also, because every Monad is all-light, all-life, all-knowing, like its source it cannot directly experience what is not perfect, what is not operating in the same very high dimensional levels. To overcome this difficulty all the Monads (and there were and are millions of them) created souls as extensions of themselves to be their vehicle and representative for learning, experiencing and growing. One of these extensions is *your* soul and so the Monad which gave it life is directly connected to you. Indeed, it is a part of you.

THE SOUL

Your soul is always a non-physical energy – one without a body – but, unlike your Monad from which it is born, which is always pure light and love because it is a reflection of God, the light of which your soul is made up is impressionable, and the brilliance of the light, its quality and clarity can change according to the experience of your soul. Remember, the soul was brought into existence to have experiences and, because it has been 'stepped down' from God, it is able to work in lower dimensions inaccessible to your Monad.

Being non-physical a soul can have its experiences directly without the need for a physical body when it is in a place of high and pure spirituality such as the planet Venus, but if it chooses to experience what it is to be in much denser matter, such as on Earth, then, just as the Monad created your soul to help its purpose, it is necessary for your soul to create its own offshoot with a lower vibration able to tolerate that density for its purpose.[1] Soul offshoots or extensions, then, are human beings, bodies with personalities living in the world of matter on Earth. One of them is you, the person you see in the mirror every day and, again, your soul is the bridge between you and God.

THE PERSONALITY

So, through your personality you are the physical reflection of the soul and have at the heart of you the divine spark, the Monad, which brought your soul into being. Incidentally, your personality is more than your qualities and charisma. In spiritual terms and as used in this book, your personality incorporates your physical body, your emotional body and your mental body.

You are a key vehicle for learning and experiencing on behalf of God and each time you are born on Earth it is for specific learning experiences to help your soul and through it the divine.

97

It sounds good, doesn't it? The catch in all of this is that if you remembered all that your soul and Monad know or have ever experienced it would make your chosen task only too easy, for you would know everything, past, present and future, and all your decision-making in your life on Earth would be determined by that insider knowledge. As a result, when you come into incarnation on Earth you are required to have no memory of anything that has gone before so that all that you experience is the result of your choice and free will. I have talked about this earlier, as you may recall.

This is quite a challenge and sometimes people get so caught up in the world of matter they cannot free themselves from it and become separated from their spiritual self for a very long time. On the other hand, learning through being in a human body offers the greatest opportunities anywhere for soul growth and so the chance to incarnate is prized. The hope is always that the learning and experiencing and soul expansion leads to remembering your spiritual heritage, your connection with God, for when this happens your beliefs and attitudes change inevitably and you are fast-forwarded towards your spiritual destiny.

Every spiritual step forward increases the brilliance of your light, which then expands the sea of Light which is God. This is why understanding the part you play, your lineage, is so important to assist that process. That is what I wish to do through this book – to help you see the truth about who and what you are as spirit, as soul and as a human being, to see the totality of you and to help you grow.

THE EVOLUTION OF THE SOUL

It is worth repeating that your soul is the bridge between you as a human being and God, through the Monad, and the desire of your soul is to experience every aspect of being human in order to evolve and become pure light. It takes many lifetimes to do this, as Chapter Three on Reincarnation explained.

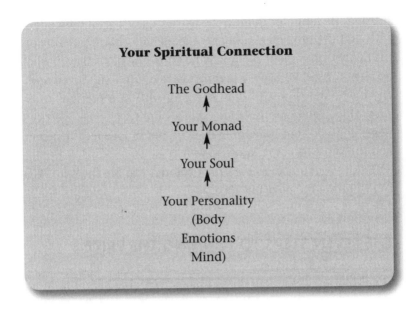

Your Spiritual Connection

The Godhead
↑
Your Monad
↑
Your Soul
↑
Your Personality
(Body
Emotions
Mind)

I talked about karma in detail earlier but, briefly here, I will remind you that everything that you do leaves a karmic footprint which is reflected directly on the soul. When you abuse power, the soul is affected like an illness in the body which must then be healed at a later time. When you use power wisely and altruistically it brings, literally, light upon the soul which stays for ever. So, your learning experiences on Earth result in karma, light and dark, and the soul's development depends on how you heal negative karma and accrue good karma. This is why how you live and behave are so very important because your spiritual development is dependent upon your soul's development, which depends upon how you live as a human being.

When your soul has completed its mission of learning and is light, its need to experience through being human ceases and it unites back to its source – your Monad and God – joyful in the knowledge that it has contributed to the expansion of the Light of the divine force, as well as having graduated with honour. This is the goal, the prize. It is like an explorer who is sent off on a special mission. He longs for home as he battles against great difficulties, tests and the unknown, and also experiences amazing events on his many voyages, but eventually he knows he has achieved what he went for and he is given permission to return to his loved ones, those who are closest to him, bringing with him precious treasures. Huge celebrations ensue, it is a hero's welcome. He need never go back – but sometimes he does, out of love for the people and the lands he got to know so well.

This is your story. You are the explorer, you are the hero. You too will have the prize one day.

THE SEVEN STEPS TO WINNING THE PRIZE

The evolution of the soul doesn't happen in a haphazard fashion, but as with everything to do with God's Plan it is carefully managed and regulated. In summary, you are trying to expand your consciousness and this is achieved through what you do and how you behave. The more you refine your rough edges the more spiritual you become.

While you are going through your Earth experiences the process of soul expansion happens in seven stages of learning, or initiations, which everyone must undertake when they are ready. Another way of looking at it is to see yourself moving up from one class at school to the next. Your rate of progress through these stages depends on how quickly you learn your Earth lessons and it varies for everybody. So, the power-hungry despot who is caught up in a long karmic cycle of corruption is going to take longer on the second set of lessons than the person who has the same experience initially but who learns comparatively quickly what is necessary about what *not* to do or be, and what *is*, and then can move on to the next learning challenge.

Let's look now at what these initiations, tests or lessons are, and what they mean for you.

Lesson 1 – Self-control

Dimension: third (the physical plane)[2]
Chakra: first (base) which deals with the physical
Colour: red

Look around you for a moment. Look at the world, the culture of which you are a part, perhaps even your own immediate environment. Listen to the news on the media, read the papers ... so much of what you see and hear about, or experience, is a reminder of what this lesson is all about – moderation and restraint, self-control if you like, particularly to do with the physical.

Obesity, greed, drunkenness, gambling, knives, violence, abuse, easy sex, drugs: they are all symptoms of a society that has much to learn about self-control over the physical aspects of life, those to do with the body and self-discipline. It is remarkable that not so very long ago there would have been great stigma associated with much of what is prevalent today, like the youth crime and drink culture, ASBOs, no-go areas in towns and cities, lack of community spirit and addiction. Of course, society never has been perfect and attitudes and ethics change over cycles of time, but the present one seems to have gone backwards rather than advanced in recent history in learning its first spiritual lesson. This is a sign that very many people are still unconscious in the spiritual kindergarten, waiting for their soul to awaken.

These uncontrolled behaviour patterns in individuals and cultures are evidence of how in the world of materialism you can become separated from your soul. When this happens you are motivated by a self-centred attitude to life. Your comfort and well-being and self-gratification are paramount and you do not care particularly about the welfare or interests of others.

Your helpers in Spirit, who are constantly striving to help you reconnect with your soul, to remember your spiritual roots and to grow, give you opportunity after opportunity to be more thoughtful, to care for your body better, to be more restrained in how you behave and, as soon as you respond, then the soul begins to stir.

You are on the path to remembering your spiritual essence and have passed the first test.

How might this apply to you?

- Do you drink too much? Take drugs regularly?

- Are you overweight through over-eating? Do you care?

- Are you addicted to sex?

- How much do you gossip?

- Do you spend a lot of your spare time watching television, playing computer games or otherwise distracting yourself?

- When was the last time you gave to charity?

- When was the last time you put someone else's needs ahead of your own? (Don't count family.)

- Do you genuinely care about the homeless and starving in Africa? If you do, what have you done about it?

You will be able to tell from your response to these questions how far you are still practising the first test, and which areas need to be strengthened.

Lesson 2 – Desires and emotions

Dimension: fourth (astral or emotional plane)
Chakra: second (sacral)
Colour: orange

Many of the people who approach me for help are working on the second test, which is one of the hardest of all the human tests and which can take many lifetimes to pass. It is all about overcoming your anxieties, your emotions, your desires and your attachments. If you are struggling with issues to do with fear (of poverty or lovelessness for example) and material desire, or if you crave wealth, beauty, status, designer clothes, celebrity or power, then probably you are working on this second initiation which applies to control over your emotions, attachments and neediness. Addiction can come into this category when it is based on an emotional lack.

My client, Liz, was and is a lovely woman who wanted only to be married and have a family, but found that every man she attracted to her eventually left her. Her longing for a loving relationship and her fear of loneliness brought about exactly the situation she so desperately wanted to avoid. So, her fears and emotions drove away any man who came close to her and her spiral of despair deepened.

Not realising the beauty she possessed externally and internally, she began to believe her appearance was the problem and that if she sorted that out all her problems would be solved. She spent a lot of money that she could not afford on plastic surgery, make-up and clothes, and as her debts mounted so also did her wine consumption. Eventually she sought help to get her life back into proportion.

Liz is an excellent example of someone working on the second test. When she was able to understand what she was doing and where this pattern of behaviour within herself came from – which included some karmic influences – she was able consciously change her outlook and behaviour and move on.

By practising the guidance given in Chapter One about developing your spirituality through the way you live, the way you think, the way you are, you will find you are much better able to move through this test successfully when you are ready.

How far does this lesson apply to you?

- How much do you worry about money?

- Have you had plastic surgery? Why?

- What is your greatest fear? Why?

- Do you always wear the latest fashion? Do you have to?

- What is your greatest ambition? Why?

- What can't you live without? Why?

- How often do you get angry? Depressed?

- Are you moody?

- Do you feel free?

- How joyful are you?

- Is your life filled with abundance?

If you cannot answer positively to the last three questions then you are working on this second test. Your replies to the earlier questions will be an indication as to what particular patterns of behaviour you are strengthening. Indeed, some of your answers may relate also to the first test about self-control.

Lesson 3 – The mind

Dimension: fifth (mental plane)
Chakra: third (solar plexus)
Colour: yellow

Having struggled with the second test for so long, the third and fourth lessons often follow quickly, perhaps in the same lifetime depending on the efforts and achievements of each individual. The third deals with controlling your thoughts and chatterbox mind and we looked at this in some detail in Chapter One. I told you then that, for me, learning to detach from my mind and to get it under control has been one of the hardest lessons of my journey. I had a strong mind which was always questioning, challenging, judging, criticising and generally undermining me, and the peace and relief that ensued when I managed to pass this test was enormous; it changed my life.

Not only does it greatly assist, literally, your peace of mind, but this initiation is also a significant one in that, having mastered control of your physical, emotional and now mental state, your soul is in the driving seat. Rather than being driven by the perceived needs of the personality, you are working in co-operation with your soul and you are a highly evolved spiritual being. Your personality is part of your soul and your light, the glow of your spirituality, is starting to be visible.

It is not until this point that you are of a sufficiently high vibrational and light level to able to sense your Monad, that spark which connects you directly to God and receive occasional guidance directly from it. Until now your guidance has been from your soul, acting as the intermediary between you, as the personality, and the divine. Now it has changed, dramatically: not only is your soul at the wheel as you drive through life, but you have begun a profound reconnection to the higher realms of God.

Let's look to see if your soul is now the driver for you: when thinking about the questions that follow, contrast how you are now with how you were a year ago.

- Is your chatterbox mind quieter?

- Do you look younger?

- Do you have peace of mind, usually?

- Are you free from desire and attachment?

- Is there anything you crave?

- Do you feel more knowledgeable about spiritual truths?

- Does your life feel balanced? How much love is there in it?

Lesson 4 – Suffering or renunciation

Dimension: sixth (soul or Buddhic plane)
Chakra: fourth (heart)
Colour: pink or green

The name of this fourth test sounds quite depressing and it is true that this period of learning can be one of sacrifice and great difficulty, but also of magnificent achievement. It used to be that it took one or more lifetimes to pass the lesson and sometimes to do so it was necessary to lose your life in a dramatic or traumatic way. Jesus passed this test, not for the first time, while on the Cross, which is why the test is sometimes known as the Crucifixion. As a great soul, even though He had undergone all the Earth initiations before in previous lifetimes, He returned to inspire and teach through word and example, which included undergoing all the initiations that humans would take over time, including the Crucifixion initiation.

The purpose of the test is to learn to give up your self-centred priorities and the demands of the personality in order to devote yourself to your service to Spirit, which is now all-important to you. While undergoing this test the experience of 'the dark night of the soul' can seem very real. The process is unique for everyone. Some people have a breakdown or a physical illness, some people have a death in the family, some people may lose much if not all of their money or possessions, others may lose their job and have to start something completely new. For some brave souls it may mean losing everything.

On the other hand, it does not have to be, at all, that the learning comes from a catastrophic event, but for everyone undergoing this test there is a sense of emotional distress, sadness, depression or an innate emotional discomfort which cannot be defined.

However it is experienced, when it passes and you are able to move on from it, you will feel to a certain degree reborn and something new will be in your life and yourself, whether it is a new house, new clothes, a new job or a new attitude. It is a time of liberation and to be welcomed as a very major spiritual achievement. Some people are conscious of a feeling of joy and inner peace at this point in their journey, while for others this is yet to come, or merely intermittent.

Spiritually speaking, the reason why this test is so painful is because it involves a major change to your relationship with your soul. Until now, for lifetime after lifetime your soul has been your guide and mentor, your faithful and best friend. At this point, however, its role as intermediary between you as a human being and your divine links is no longer needed because you have got to the point where you can connect directly with your Monad constantly and permanently rather than just occasionally.

Some people believe that the soul, at this point, is burnt up and destroyed, but this is not the case. It exists still and remains your light meter, the indicator of the growing brilliance of your light. What happens is that your soul merges with your Monad and allows the Monad, that part of you which is Spirit, to be your guide and teacher from now on. Even though the integration with the Monad is what you have been working towards for an eternity, there is much sorrow when the soul is assimilated for it is like the loss of everything you have known and held dear. When Jesus on the Cross said, 'My God, my God, why has thou forsaken me?', He was referring to what He thought was the loss of His soul.

For some time after this momentous event you will feel great sadness and the change will reflect itself in your own personal world – 'as within, so without' – and this is when physical loss, adjustment or suffering in some form or other can occur. I stress again that passing this test does not have to be hugely turbulent as it did once upon a time, but however it manifests itself, you will feel it.

After a period of adjustment you will feel more strongly aware of your spiritual self and of those from the world of Spirit who are helping you. Your knowledge and self-understanding will have deepened and you may wish to work overtly and publicly as a spiritual teacher or healer in some capacity. You may feel drawn to read more spiritual books and to attend courses and talks more than ever before, or alternatively you may wish to spend some time in retreat or private contemplation and meditation. You will feel different even if your outer life is much the same as it was – though the likelihood is that it, too, will change.

Lesson 5 – Revelation

Dimension: seventh (plane of spiritual consciousness)
Chakra: fifth (throat)
Colour: sky blue

The Revelation initiation follows the fourth test very rapidly and is to do with the integration of your soul merger with Spirit which has just occurred. It is the first cosmic test, even though you have taken it on the Earth plane, and it enables you to develop your telepathic and sometimes psychic gifts. At this time you are evolving rapidly as a spiritual being and accumulating and remembering much wisdom and information. It is as if the veils have come away from your eyes and you can see. Moreover, for the first time you are given a glimpse of the choices of cosmic specialisation available to you for your future spiritual service.

You are very close to completing the ascension process, which occurs at the next two initiations.

Lesson 6 – Ascension and decision

Dimension: eighth (plane of total interconnectedness)
Chakra: sixth (third eye)
Colour: indigo

At this time your expansion of consciousness is continuing to develop quickly. You are not learning Earth lessons as such, rather tying up loose ends to do with the personality and perhaps are being given reminders of some of the key lessons that you incarnated to learn about. Now you are aware of the great spiritual wisdoms (known as the Universal Laws and described in Chapter Eight) and are living by them, and as you do so the brilliance of your light continues to increase until you have reached the point of ascension and have passed the sixth test. You are now a creature of such spiritual luminosity that you are liberated from the requirement to be reborn on Earth again, unless you choose to return to help the Earth and humanity out of your love for them.

The number of people who are of this exalted level on Earth are few, but they are amongst us sometimes anonymously, sometimes venerated publicly as being great spiritual leaders. Whatever their status they are recognisable, by anyone with eyes to see, for the light radiating from them, their wisdom, their compassion and the quality of their energy.

Ascension means that you are able to work in many dimensions and are as much connected with the spiritual realms as you are with your physical world, which exists in the third dimension. It used to be that ascension meant that you left the Earth plane altogether, a master returning to be pure spirit, but now the likelihood is that you will continue to live on Earth as you did before, to complete your mission and service looking as you always did, with your own unique personality and skills, except with an even stronger glow of Spirit within you. You are filled with joy and love for all, total spirituality in action and an example and inspiration to many.

Meanwhile, in anticipation of further cosmic initiations and your spiritual path to come, you are required now to choose what spiritual work you wish to do in the service of God. There is no turning back from the decision you make at this time, which is why it is called the Initiation of Decision. It is of crucial importance for it will decide your future spiritual journey.

Lesson 7 – Merger

Dimension: ninth (plane of God, divinity, the essence)
Chakra: seventh (crown)
Colour: violet

This is the last of the initiations you can take on Earth and it is a continuation of the spiritual development and refinement that has been going on since the fifth test. Now your soul is filled with light and you have merged with the divine. You are connected with all that is anywhere, including God. You are still human, but with an ever-growing radiance which is eye-catching and magnetic without being strange.

There are two further initiations that you will take after this seventh test and they occur on the cosmic planes. It is unlikely you will be in body when you take them.

After the ninth initiation you will continue your spiritual evolution but in other cosmic realms, each with their own high dimensional levels far from Earth, reaching ultimately to the Source or God. So, your spiritual journey never stops and the tests and challenges continue far beyond the Earth plane, however evolved your soul.

Sometimes certain initiations are undergone simultaneously, rather like a student studying several A levels at one time. For example, if the lesson about attachment to having money is taking you a long time to assimilate, it may be this second initiation will continue to be learned while you are also being taught how to keep your 'chatterbox' mind under control and in balance, which is part of the third initiation.

All the Earth lessons are achievable and you will pass every test eventually, though it will take many, many lifetimes for you to reach the seventh and final stages of planetary learning. Unlike being at school, you move through the different levels at your own pace depending on your soul make-up and sometimes you have to take a particular test several times over, even if you have passed it already, in situations where you have forgotten what you have learnt from one lifetime to the next.

A friend of mine, Sally, told me once about a very realistic dream she had had while asleep. She was alone in a library and she knew this was a place where she came often to study. There were big French windows in the room and she was drawn to go to them and look out. It was night time, but outside the windows was her dog who had died a few years before and which she had loved very much. He was jumping up and wagging his tail, delighted to see her, looking at her and then at the scene behind him. Beyond him, Sally saw a landscape of great beauty, a night-time view of heaven on Earth. She longed to go through the windows to meet her dog and go with him into this land of mystery and magic, but when she tried to open them the way was barred. She had to stay where she was. She awoke with the feeling of the greatest longing and sadness upon her heart, which returns to her whenever she remembers her experience.

Sally is convinced her dream was real and that the library is where her soul goes to be taught. Her dog awaits her and when she has completed her service on Earth she will be allowed to go through the window to rejoin him and return to heaven.

You are unlikely to know when a test is over – there is not an exam or formal ceremony – except you may notice a change in how you feel and in the nature of the lessons placed before you. Suddenly, perhaps, your long-standing concerns about money don't exist any more but instead you find relationship issues becoming prominent in your life. A great deal occurs when you are asleep that you remember nothing about: your soul travels and learns and experiences very much including, sometimes, injections of spiritual energy and light which can be associated with the completion of an important spiritual lesson and the resulting expansion of spiritual consciousness. This is why you may wake up sometimes feeling tired, or with a dim or strong memory of vivid dreams. Those apparent dreams can be a spiritual reality.

The initiatory process is longer for some people than for others, depending on their spiritual commitment and their karmic situation. Anyone who is working actively to develop himself or herself spiritually, or just wishes to know more about spirituality – such as through reading this and other such books – is probably on an initiatory fast-track. The process after level three can be rapid and many tests can be undertaken successfully in one lifetime for those who are 'awake'.

Remember, each series of tests is given to you in order to strengthen those aspects of your soul and personality that need it. Everybody, however, gets there in the end. Everybody earns their prize. You will too, whether it is in this lifetime or one yet to come.

Here is a summary of the lessons you take on Earth:

Initiation	Learning	Dimension	Plane	Chakra	Colour
First	Self-control	Third	Physical	Base	Red
Second	Desires and emotions	Fourth	Astral	Sacral	Orange
Third	Mental control	Fifth	Mental	Solar plexus	Yellow
Fourth	Suffering (soul merger)	Sixth	Soul	Heart	Pink or green
Fifth	Revelation (start of the ascension process)	Seventh	Spiritual consciousness	Throat	Sky blue
Sixth	Decision	Eighth	Total inter-connectedness	Third eye	Indigo
Seventh	Merger	Ninth	The essence of God	Crown	Violet

YOUR CHOICES FOR COSMIC SPIRITUAL SERVICE

When you have passed the sixth initiatory test you will choose a particular way of working and studying at a much higher level of consciousness than before, rather like choosing what to study for a university mastership. For most people, their chosen path will mean they no longer live physically on Earth, unless they have chosen to help the planet in which case they may either assist Earth and humanity in body or from a higher non-physical realm.

Whatever your choice of spiritual service, it will determine the nature of your spiritual specialisation for ever – it is rather like a young doctor choosing what area of medical expertise they wish to be in, in the knowledge it will apply, probably, for his or her whole career. The choice here will last for eternity and will lead you eventually to the ultimate Godhead.

Very little is known or has been written about these choices and what we have, besides being limited, is cryptic. The theosophical writer and channel Alice Bailey has written more than anyone else on the subject and a few people like Dr Joshua Stone, author of *The Complete Ascension Manual* and other works, have produced useful guidance based on her work.

This is my understanding of the choices that will be available to you. I have made them as simple for you to understand as I can, but I recognise they are complex still![3] I include this brief information about them for the sake of completeness because, having shown you the start of the soul journey, you may wish to know 'what happens next'. In fact, the soul journey never ends. As soul and spirit you will work in ever more cosmic realms, expanding your light and the light of God, a vital part of God's team for ever.

Your choices of cosmic spiritual service are as follows:

Choice 1: Spiritual service on Earth

There is a group of highly evolved non-physical beings who devote their efforts to helping the evolution of Earth, humanity and all the planet's other inhabitants. Some of these spiritual

Masters are helping *you* too, one or two in particular whom you may know by name one day. All of these Ones have chosen this first path. Only a small number of Masters are allowed to do this work, just enough to get the job done. They, like you, will have spent many lifetimes on Earth and their love for the planet and for humanity has caused them to wish to remain in service here even after their ascension.

If this is your choice also one day, you will be required to make a further decision about the nature of your Earth service in order to determine which one of the four kingdoms of nature (mineral, plant, animal and human) you will assist in particular.

After a certain period of time during which you will continue to grow and evolve, you will move on to other more cosmic work, thus creating a vacancy for others.

Choice 2: Service relating to science and spiritual energy

If you are drawn to work on this path, you are likely to be someone who is fascinated by science, knowledge and research. You will be working with information, ideas and facts, also manipulating energy of a very specific kind. The magnetic influence of Libra on this path is strong and you will be directing and controlling the movement and placement of this and other magnetic energies.

Choice 3: Service relating to other planets

Very few people are chosen for this specialist path, which is the opportunity to train to work on a particular planet in the solar system and, eventually, perhaps to be the Divine Presence Itself for that planet. In terms of time as we understand it, it may take thousands and thousands of man-years to reach that exalted status.

Selection requires an ability to work with cosmic colour, vision and sound, and to have an interest in and understanding of the process of the expansion of consciousness. It has been called, rightly, 'the science of the soul' and 'divine psychology'.

Choice 4: Service to assist cosmic evolution

There is much mystery over this path and very little is known, even though the majority of humankind enter this path. The work is to do with Sirius, the brightest star in our night sky. Sirius itself is believed to be a major transmission point of spiritual energy directed at Earth and it has connections also with the Pleiades and the Sun.

Because this is the fourth choice of service, with three choices coming before and after it, it has a key part to play as an inter-connector between all the path choices, like a bridge.

If you are on this path you will be dealing with cosmic evolution and the Universal Mind.

Choice 5: Service relating to the dissemination of the Qualities of God

This path concerns energy, also knowledge and, most importantly, the qualities of God. If you make this choice you will have a clear understanding of and attraction to cosmic stability and magnetic balance as part of your work to disseminate the qualities and energies of God throughout the cosmos.

Esoterically, this path concerns 'the Rays' which are discussed later in Chapter Six.

Choice 6: Service relating to the Path of God

The information available on the two final paths is minimal, because the implications are so huge. They approach the heart of God and what is beyond God, and for us as humans with limited understanding of the cosmic worlds, the enormity of it all is almost incomprehensible. Those who are on these last two paths have a level of cosmic consciousness which is unimaginable.

The Path of the Deity is one that is very difficult for most people to access; it really is for those who are most highly evolved, very special souls indeed. Most individuals who reach it do so via the fifth path and even then they have to spend time working in the angelic realms before they can do this work.

The work of these great Lives is to do with inner sight, cosmic vision and psychic abilities, and a special ability to work with certain cosmic vibrations. It is the Path of Light.

Choice 7: Service relating to the Greater God

If you are evolved enough to be on this path, you will be working in the highest dimensions. You will be an intimate of the Greater God and doing His will. You will be dealing with the relationship between the solar system, planet Earth and the universe, and helping non-sacred planets to gain sacred status. You will be managing the inflow of divine energies from the furthest reaches of the cosmos. It is impossible to say more.

Exercise 5: Identify your current Earth lessons

It may help you to know which of the lessons described in this chapter you are learning now. One or two of the descriptions and examples I gave you will, perhaps, have resonated with you as you read about them. This exercise will clarify further how you stand with your spiritual development and where to place your focus if you wish to help your spiritual growth.

Do not have any expectations! It is natural to want to be doing your spiritual mastership rather than kicking your heels in the playground, but please remember that the majority of people haven't even started kindergarten yet. So, if you find you are learning lessons to do with your physical life, do not be disappointed or judge yourself negatively. You are doing well and whatever you are working on is for a reason. Also, you may be working on your dissertation at level four while working on lesson one at the same time.

Find a place and time where you will not be disturbed and

---

when you are not over-tired. Allow yourself at least half an hour. Read the information about the different initiations before you begin, so it is fresh in your mind.

If you wish, light a candle or burn some incense to indicate to your higher self that you are going to be working spiritually.

Set your intention, which is to identify which are the main qualities you are learning to strengthen now. Ensure you are fully protected, as you have been taught.

The exercise

- Close your eyes and feel yourself relax. Focus on your breathing as your mind becomes calm and quiet.

- If you wish, invite your helpers in Spirit to be present to assist you.

- Now, see yourself in a cinema, waiting for a film to start. You are the only person in the audience, though you are aware of loving energies all around you.

- The film starts and it is all about you. It is a film of your life as you are now and it is looking at different aspects of your personality.

- Look at the screen. You are watching yourself acting out your greatest learnings to do with your life as a human, seeing what is most out of balance, out of control a little, an aspect of your physical lifestyle that you are embarrassed about or ashamed of or that you regret. DO NOT BE JUDGEMENTAL. If you know what the significant lesson is here, then you can do something more about it.

- Let the image fade and now see yourself on screen sitting on a chair doing nothing. Ask your screen self, 'What is your greatest fear?'

- Then, 'What can you not live without?'

- Then 'What is your greatest learning?'

Your screen self will give you an answer to each question.

- Allow the image to fade and return to your chair and every-day surroundings.

- Take your spiritual journal and make a note of what you saw and heard. It is likely that you will have received at least one piece of information about yourself. Ponder on what you have learnt and what you wish to do about it.

- Thank your spiritual helpers before you leave, ensure your chakras are closed down and that you have put protection around yourself.

Chapter Five

The Cycles of Light and Dark

Having looked at the magnificence of the journey of your soul in Chapter Four, I invite you now to consider with me some of the spiritual concepts relating to cycles of time, energy and spirituality. While they have implications throughout the cosmos I will be keeping the discussion rather closer to home, looking at the impact they have upon our world and you personally. They are important, and understanding why they are important, what they are and what they mean will help to develop your sense of your part in God's Plan, your spiritual heritage and influences, and may also expand your consciousness considerably.

Let me begin by looking at one of the ancient spiritual beliefs to do with the energy of God and a particular aspect of how that energy applies to Earth. It is to do with 'the breath of God', which is both a metaphor and a truth to do with the coming and going of different belief systems over thousands of years.

THE BREATH OF GOD EXPLAINED

Spiritual wisdom states that when God *exhales* He is sending out His spiritual energy, His light, through time and space. The further it goes out, the more it becomes diluted through its gradual descent from the sublime world of spirit, heaven you could say, to the dark world of matter. When God *inhales*, He is drawing His energy back to the Godhead, where Spirit is at its strongest because it is where He resides.

Each in-breath and out-breath represents a spiritual cycle and they balance each other out perfectly. The beginning of the out-breath cycle is a time of great spirituality because it is closest to God and its end is a time when spirituality is obscured, hidden under a heavy mantle of materialism because it is furthest away from the Godhead. By the end of the second cycle, which is the in-breath, the energy is one of light and purity once again as it returns to the Source.

There is a further aspect to do with these cycles, which is relevant to you. You see, as God exhales, He is sending you, me and humanity further and further into the world of matter, to experience that world, to learn and to grow – do you see how this ties in with what I wrote about the purpose of your soul's journey in Chapter Four? When you have learned your important lessons in Earth school, then God begins to draw you back to Him when you are ready. You have your cycles of experiencing dark and light, so does humanity and so does our planet.

Putting it very simply you could say that, on Earth, there are long cycles of love and altruism (the 'we' approach) which gradually over time are replaced by cycles of selfishness (the 'I' approach). The 'I' cycle that predominates in our world now will change, inevitably, to be superseded by loving kindness once again.

The following diagrams show you what I mean.

Out-breath of God (cycle of descent into matter)

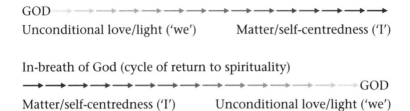

GOD
Unconditional love/light ('we')   Matter/self-centredness ('I')

In-breath of God (cycle of return to spirituality)

GOD
Matter/self-centredness ('I')   Unconditional love/light ('we')

THE GOLDEN AGES

About 26,000 years ago a significant cycle of time and energy began on Earth and as a result the ethos of profound spirituality that had been pre-eminent began to change. God, you could say, started to exhale and man began to experience more and more all there was to know about being in matter.

That particular cycle is drawing to an end now. As it does, you can see that most of mankind, particularly in the Western world, has become caught up in a world of materialism and self-centredness – very much the 'I' mentality, and as far from the spiritual ethos that existed at the start of the cycle as it can be. As the cycle completes, imminently, we can look forward to a new 26,000 year cycle (God's in-breath) which will bring back a longing for and an insistence on a spiritual way of life once again. The cycle ahead of us is called the New Golden Age. You will be a part of this New Age. You already are.

Just as there is a pause every time you yourself breathe in and out, so also there will be a pause between these two great cycles and this pause will be a significant moment in eternity. The year when this momentous event will take place is 2012 – so close to taking place that I believe we are in the pause period now.

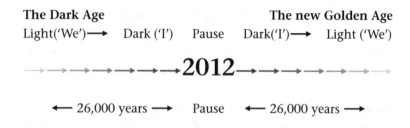

The Dark Age

The new Golden Age

Light('We')⟶ Dark ('I') Pause Dark('I')⟶ Light ('We')

⟶ ⟶ ⟶ ⟶ ⟶ **2012**⟶ ⟶ ⟶ ⟶ ⟶

⟵ 26,000 years ⟶   Pause   ⟵ 26,000 years ⟶

THE SIGNIFICANCE OF 2012

There is a big difference in people's understanding of what 2012 means. The majority believe that it will be a year like any other, though with exceptional highlights in certain places. In the UK, for example, the Olympics are scheduled to take place in London and there should be an election for Mayor, while in the US, France, Finland and Mexico presidential elections are expected. For most people there is no awareness at all that we are approaching a hugely significant time which could bring about a pivotal change to the planet and to humanity.

Other people are more aware of the momentous spiritual possibilities to come, but take a gloomy approach. Some commentators think that 2012 will herald a peak oil catastrophe which will result in permanent blackouts as the electricity networks fail across the world.[1] In certain quarters there is a belief that there will be an alien invasion at that time; that the Earth's magnetic poles will shift catastrophically; or that the world will come to an end as the result of a nuclear world war or collision with a comet. Other people have a more positive attitude and believe that 2012 will see the Second Coming of Christ, the Buddha or another great spiritual leader.

Certainly, astronomically 2012 is predicted to be a year of significance: at the solstice on 21 December 2012, the sun will align with the Milky Way galactic centre and this will come about as a result of the slow wobbling of the Earth upon its axis, otherwise known as 'the precession of the equinoxes'. One wobble takes about 26,000 years and so a galactic alignment such as this occurs only once every 26,000 years – which takes us neatly back to the great cycles of time and associated spiritual change that I have discussed above. It is said that the Mayan calendar, which predicts both the alignment itself on that date and a resulting change of human consciousness, ends then as it marks the completion of one era and the ushering in of another.[2]

My own sense, which is shared by many other spiritual teachers and guides, is that the solstices in June and December 2012, and the time leading up to them, will be significant but not in a totally calamitous way. There will be a realignment of our planet which will result in some earth changes, such as volcanic activity and perhaps flooding in places, but humanity will not be wiped out. Indeed, as we are entering the 'pause' period now between the two cycles, evidence of these changes is clear already through extreme and disruptive weather patterns in different parts of the world.

Most importantly I believe that this period leading up to and including 2012 will change the consciousness of humanity, as the Mayans have foretold, as a result of world events and that a new era of spirituality *will* begin.

This will be the start of the next Golden Age. *This* is the Second Coming that has been predicted and longed for by Christians, Buddhists and many other faiths and beliefs, and the result, I believe strongly, will be unconditional love in the hearts of men and women everywhere.

THE TEMPLE OF LIGHT

The last Golden Age, which ended 26,000 years ago, has been called the time of the Temple of Light. The Temple is a metaphor for an era when spiritual values prevailed upon Earth, when the emphasis was upon living in peace and harmony within a society where altruism, kindness and common sense were the norm and where leaders were chosen for their spiritual wisdom, lineage and example.

There was a physical Temple also or, rather, there were in fact 12 Temples of Light which were great spiritual centres situated in certain places around the world, the energies of which together covered the Earth with a mantle of divine energy. Humanity felt connected and at one with God, the cosmos and all that lived on Earth alongside them. Everything was in balance.

When the era of Light and Love changed as the new era of darkness encroached, and as humanity became increasingly forgetful of its spiritual links and responsibilities, the Temple, literally and figuratively, began to crumble and to be forgotten. Those priests and servers who had tended the sacred flames for so long sadly withdrew the spiritual secrets and wisdoms that were beginning to be misused and ridiculed and hid them in places where they could be resurrected when humanity was ready to receive them once again. Many of these priests were found, taken and persecuted for their beliefs and spiritual knowledge and practices.

With the imminence of the next great cycle, those guardians of the secrets are among us once again and are rebuilding the Temple now, ready to fulfil their mission and fulfil with you the purpose for which humanity came to Earth in the first place – to learn, to grow, to expand the light individually and as a group and to help the planet on her own soul journey to ascension and then sacred status – I talk about this further in the Epilogue. This is why it is so exciting and important to be alive at this time and be aware of our spiritual heritage and purpose.

As well as the priests of old, many other people who were present in the last Golden Age are gathering on the planet once again to be part of the rebirth of the new era. You who are reading this book may well have been among them and are here now to assist and support the important work of bringing peace and harmony to Earth. It is no coincidence that you have this book in your hand – there is no such thing as coincidence – and it may be that reading these words will stir your memories and be a catalyst for remembering and moving forward.

How do you feel about what I have written here? Some of you will feel your heart stir, a sense of longing, sadness, excitement – a strong indication you have a connection to those events I have described. If you do, don't be surprised by dreams and memories that may come to you, or if you are drawn to certain books or teachers that may enhance your awareness of your spiritual lineage. If it feels alien or untrue, then please move on light-heartedly. I am happy to accept that not everyone will share my beliefs and understanding of these and other ancient events and wisdoms.

LIGHT AND DARK

I wish to consider now a different aspect of the cycles of light and dark and to consider how the light and, particularly in this section, the dark have been used through time positively and negatively and how they impact on you today.

The divine nature of light and dark
Light is Spirit, God is Light. The light and warmth of the sun, which governs our solar system and our planet, provide food, energy and warmth and without it there could be no life on Earth. Even when the sun is not visible and where you are in the world is in darkness, the presence and influence of God can be felt in the nightlife of nature which also, directly and indirectly, depends on the light for its life and nourishment, and in the stars and the moon, light in themselves. God can be found in the darkest places and the place that is blackest can have the most light, even if you cannot see it.

Sometimes, if you meditate and reach a profound state of spiritual connection, you will find yourself in the void, a state of nothingness and yet of everything, where your breathing ceases and you are in a state of bliss. It is a moment when the world stops for you, you are nothing but spirit and all you 'see' is the deepest and most beautiful shade of black. This is the colour of God at its most intense and to be in this place is very wonderful. The darkness represents, you could say, light and dark, opposites of each other, becoming one.

The moon and darkness

There is much misunderstanding about the dark, based on old fears and prejudice, and there is a superstitious unease about the time in the month when there is no moon visible, the 'dark of the moon'. In fact, the dark moon, which occurs every month just before the new moon is visible and lasts for about three days, represents the womb of the universe and that period is a very significant opportunity to connect to the source of everything, including your own roots. It is a point of power representing pure creation, while the full moon represents the intelligence which gives life to what has been created.

The energy of the dark moon is one of deep inner wisdom and it is an energy that exists to help the evolution of the planet. At a time long ago in our history there was a shared and universal understanding of what this meant, but now it is only certain ancient cultures, tribes, societies and individuals, those people who have not lost their innate knowledge of the laws and secrets of the cosmos and the divine, who remember, comprehend and use this energy. The tribes of old did not fear darkness, because darkness to them was part of the cycle of life and in their wisdom they knew that darkness and the light create balance.

Religion, darkness and myth

The reason why so many people forgot or abandoned their knowledge of traditional understandings, such as those to do with the spiritual power of the dark, was due to the development of certain organised religions, Christianity in particular.

It did not take long for the intrinsically simple and profound teachings of Jesus, which were based on the Universal Laws, to be changed here and there by those who developed His Church with good but sometimes misguided intentions. As the expectations and requirements of the Church became more rigorous, so they became more controlling, and as the Church grew so also did the opportunity for misuse of power. Huge monies and opportunities for personal gain encouraged in certain priests and political leaders the desire to curtail the freedom of the people to honour God in the way they wished or had done for hundreds or thousands of years. The Church wished to be all-powerful and it succeeded in so being for a long time.

As part of this desire to have as many people as possible in its flock, the old pagan festivals to the sun, moon, nature spirits and to the divine were redesignated Christian festivals and for a while they were allowed to take place as they always had done. These pagan festivals took place when the sun was in a certain position at fixed points in the year – Yule at the time of the winter solstice, for example, Beltane on 1 May or Lammas on 1 August. Gradually, however, the practices themselves were taken over by the Church and the purpose, format and principle behind them became discouraged and then outlawed. Anyone practising the old ways was persecuted. Thus, the people lost the heart of their spirituality, it was taken from them, and their sense of being able to connect freely with God and nature, of being a part of the spiritual totality, was eliminated.

At the same time, the Church introduced the teaching that the darkness was dangerous and that it was associated with sinfulness and the devil unless supervised by the Church. So, went the reasoning, anyone who chose to incorporate darkness into their spiritual ritual, or who even just enjoyed being in the dark, must be doing the work of the devil. Many of the old rituals took place by night and they were rapidly brought into disrepute and then disuse as a result of the new way of thinking. It was a perfect way of creating fear and so increasing the opportunity for controlling the hearts and minds of men and women.

So, you can see that the fear of judgement and persecution and the growing belief that what the Church taught must be true caused the people to abandon their ancient practices, to seek to do what was acceptable and permissible, using daylight rather than darkness wherever possible. All the old rituals to do with the Earth and the moon and man's place in the greater cosmic scheme were gradually abandoned and forgotten except by the brave few who continued secretly, despite the dangers to them.

In this way men and women were isolated from the natural environment from which they drew their strength. All the things from which they had drawn a sense of self, of strength and purpose, were classed as wicked and any ceremony which took place, for example, at the dark of the moon, was said to be the work of Satan.

The attempts to change the traditional belief systems went even further: Adam's first wife before Eve was called Lilith and she became, through Biblical reference, scholarly interpretation and folklore, the representation of all that was evil. She was associated with the dark moon and anyone who did any form of ceremony, anything that required darkness, was deemed to have been tempted by Lilith and so to have been overtaken by Satan and they had to be stopped. In fact, Lilith represents the Divine Feminine, the counterpart of the Divine Masculine. She is the feminine aspect of God and the epitome of all that is spiritual.

Similarly, in the fifth century St Jerome translated the Bible from Hebrew into Latin (the Vulgate) and for the first time named Lucifer[3] as the principal Fallen Angel, known as Satan, who introduced evil into the world and created the first sin. Thus the modern concept of sin was created.

WORKING WITH DARKNESS

Although in many places the ancient spiritual rituals and traditions including working with darkness were driven underground, they did not die out. Druids[4], Wiccans[5] and Shamans, for example, have continued to practise their beliefs using the tools of the night or darkness for divine connection, guidance and assistance, as they have done for thousands of years in different parts of the world. Some shamanic techniques involve being buried underground for days at a time, or being blindfolded for weeks in order to heighten the shamans' sensitivity and spiritual connection. The Sacred Trust, listed in the Resources section, runs powerful and effective shamanic darkness retreats.

There is another perspective to do with working with the dark. I have referred several times in this book to cycles and balance in ourselves, in nature and beyond. Just as the dark can be used with good intentions for profound spiritual purpose, so it can also be used for ill. For centuries certain people have believed that they can call upon the dark energies associated with Satan, the devil, and evil as a source of power for themselves. They have created rituals and practices which often mimic the practices of the Church or other spiritual groups but with the intention of invoking the opposite of the Light and the Love of God for their own gain. They do their work in darkness because darkness is seen to be the home of the devil.

I do not accept there is a Satan or a devil, but I do believe in negative energy and positive energy and that each of us can make good or bad out of anything, depending on what we choose to do with it. So, a child can be loved or abused; music can be enjoyed or loathed; money can be squandered or used wisely; food can be lovingly prepared or thrown into the microwave in a packet; darkness can be used positively or negatively. If you believe there is a devil, whether you fear it or love it you can create the evidence to prove your belief to yourself. If you choose to create or work with negative energy, this is what you will achieve. It is up to you.

In the end, someone who is a Satanist is someone who is choosing the path of extreme materialism and ultimate selfishness and who will create the tools he or she needs to try to obtain what they crave. Through the power of their intentions, belief and thought they may seem, sometimes, to achieve their aims, but at great cost to their soul and karmic burden.

YOUR INNER DEMONS

You have chosen your path and your life and have created the reality in which you move in order to learn the lessons of your soul journey, the ultimate aim of which is to merge with and become Spirit and to assist the expansion of God. Every individual upon Earth similarly has also chosen their own reality and for the same reason, without exception, though it is likely most people do not know the true purpose of their life on Earth.

Let me remind you that you live on a planet where you make choices all the time in order to help you with your Earth learnings, and everything you do or that happens to you is a result of one of those choices, whether it is the time and manner in which you get up, what you put into your body, what you do with your time, or how far you pursue the path of altruism – the light – or selfishness – the dark. All actions and behaviour are an aspect of spirituality or negative materialism to a greater or lesser degree, creating 'light' or 'dark' karma each time.

There is never any right or wrong about the choice you make. If someone has chosen to experience the darker experiences of life for now, then it is because he/she has something to learn, or teach others, or perhaps to undergo for karmic reasons, and those who are affected by this have chosen so to be.

Certain individuals throughout our history have become notorious for their brutality, arrogance or corruption. However dark the soul, or seemingly lost, however many lifetimes a soul has been mired in the darkness of matter, even for these people there is always the opportunity eventually to return to the light and there are messengers on hand to assist this transition if and when the soul is willing. Sometimes they have to shout loudly! But if the message or reminder is not heard or accepted, the messengers and guides in the world of spirit wait with love and compassion for the time that it will be, whether it is in this lifetime or many lifetimes hence. Whatever your choice about your path at any particular point in time, it is perfect, and you will be offered as much help as possible to assist you to choose most appropriately.

It is important to bear in mind that humans are at differing stages of development. The majority are still battling to learn and overcome issues of the personality – body, emotions and mind. As you have learnt, many people have issues to do with violence, abuse, obesity, drink, drugs, sex – issues to do with the body. The emotional challenge, the second test of the soul's journey on Earth, is the most widespread among mankind today, epitomised by a craving for possessions, power, good looks, security, money – the materialistic 'I' approach. Fear manifesting as anger, jealousy, possessiveness and so on, is the factor underlying these preoccupations and obsessions. The third lesson to do with the mind is also a hard one to learn, in which rationality and logic may be in conflict with your heart and your intuition.

These negative characteristics of body, mind and personality are your darker side, your inner demons, and they can be a major challenge for you. It is part of your initiatory process to experience, learn and then move through them when you are ready, as I have discussed at length already in the previous chapter. This can take many, many lifetimes, but by the end of this process your soul will be co-operating with your personality as opposed to being obscured by it and your demons will be gone. While much of this learning process is unconscious, it is all part of the progress of the soul. Some people take a lot longer to learn and move on than others.

The more spiritually aware you are, the more your inner demons show themselves to you to be confronted and dealt with and they can be very painful. Some people choose to believe that outside forces are manipulating the set of circumstances besetting them when these difficult times occur in their life, but that approach is often a rejection of personal responsibility to look at what is occurring within and to move through it.

If, despite the discomfort, you can recognise that your inner demons represent a wonderful opportunity to heal something important (for it is important, always) for the benefit of your soul and its journey, and you can do something about it, then it can be life changing in the most positive sense. When Jesus was in the wilderness for 40 days and nights, He was confronting and working through His own inner demons. He could not have carried out His service until he had done so.

Tony is a client and now friend who came to me for help because he had an addiction to sex. He had been to therapy, taken prescription drugs, tried different forms of healing but all without success. Because of his problem he was unable to sustain any relationship and he hated himself for his behaviour but was powerless to stop.

He approached me as a last resort to see if I could assist him at the level of the soul and spirit. Together we discovered that, over many lifetimes, he had developed karmic issues to do with love and power whereby his experiences taught him that the only way he could give or receive love was often through brutal force. This was his inner demon and his lesson was to learn about honour and compassion in relationships and what true love is.

Because his issue was so deep-rooted it took some time to help him understand fully what had been occurring and why and for him to heal it. Then, for the first time, he was able to have a relationship centred on reciprocal gifts of the heart, where he was loved for himself and where he was able to return his love wisely and considerately.

So, now you can understand what your inner demons represent, recognising them compassionately and non-judgementally as the negative aspects of the personality that you, as a spiritual being, are striving to eliminate in order to enable your soul and then your spirit, the light of God that is within you, to shine forth.

There are also, quite separate from your inner demons, the Brothers of the Shadow.

THE BROTHERS OF THE SHADOW

While your soul is a mixture of light and dark, so also there are light and dark energies impacting our world from the non-physical realms – 'As above, so below'. These energies are known as the Brothers and Sisters of the Light and the Brothers of the Shadow, terminology used also by Alice Bailey in her many esoteric books, and others. For you living on Earth at this time, the term 'Brothers of the Shadow' is a metaphor for the darker aspects of materialism which are prevalent in the world today, as well as describing certain negative cosmic energies. The energies that work with the light include your spiritual helpers and come from God. They represent the highest aspects of spirituality.

The ability of the negative cosmic energies to influence people will vary depending on the phase of the cycle humanity is part of at any one time. Their power is at its strongest when the world is at its densest point on its cycle of experiencing matter – which, as you know, is now.

As non-physical entities, the Brothers can occasionally cause indirect interference in people's lives, blocking the free flow of energies or disrupting communications, for example. Usually it is peripheral and almost unnoticeable and most certainly is not to be anticipated or feared. Unless you invoke them directly, which I would discourage strongly, they are most unlikely to have any contact with you.

LEARNING FROM THE BROTHERS OF THE SHADOW

Let me remind you again that part of the soul journey is for us to be faced with every aspect of being human, whether it is of the highest or lowest experience. So, at some point everyone will have cycles of learning about what the Brothers represent – the darkest aspects of being human.

I know that in other lifetimes I have practised extremes of cruelty, criminality and abuse of power as part of my own learning. Fortunately, since these are not karmic issues that have presented themselves for healing in this life, it looks as though the learning has been successful and I am not required to repeat them!

Just as I did, every soul will at some point choose to experience aspects of the path of the dark as part of its learning, such as through incarnating to be a black magician, a murderer or a child abuser. At its inception a soul is always of the light, from the light, and even after a lengthy period working with the Brothers of the Shadow most souls choose to return to the light – but it is a choice. Some souls are enthralled by the apparent power or glamour of a life of power and riches, however they are derived and at what expense, and become addicted.

EXPERIENCING NEGATIVITY – WHAT TO DO

Over and above your inner demons and the Brothers of the Shadow, dark energies can affect you as a result of the words and attitude of people who are close to you. If you sense that someone around you, at home or in your social group, perhaps, is not honouring, supporting or uplifting you, then as far as you are able do not spend time with them, for their negativity can be depressing or even destructive. Sometimes members of your own family can, through jealousy, possibly, or karmic residues, make life uncomfortable for you, leaving you feeling depressed or upset.

In these circumstances, on the occasions when you have to be with them because of family duty or responsibility, I suggest you place a barrier of protection around yourself, as described in the notes on meditation given earlier in the Introduction. Additionally, I suggest you avoid giving them any personal or confidential information about yourself which they can use to hurt you, however unintentionally, and this will help also.

It is very improbable that you will come across dark energies of a really serious nature, whether they are emanating from other people's negativity or from the non-physical. However, if ever you find yourself in a situation where you are aware of a presence or energy that is not of the light and that makes you a little concerned or fearful, please do not interact with it at all. If you address the energy, if you focus upon it, if you think about it you are feeding it and it will become stronger. If you ignore it, it will go away. Whatever you do, do not taunt it!

One night I was woken by the office phone that is in my house ringing several times in succession. I picked up the messages next morning. A client had called, very distressed because she was convinced a malevolent entity had attached itself to her. She claimed she could smell the odour, feel the darkness of it and said she was terrified. I called her and discovered that she had watched 'Most Haunted' (a late-night programme which investigates haunted houses, usually rather sensationally) on television the night before and that she had felt the negativity around her immediately afterwards.

On talking it through with her and then doing some work together, it was clear that she was not under any psychic or other attack, but rather had been affected by the TV programme. Her imagination had created a situation which had no basis in reality. She was much relieved and felt better immediately – and promised not to watch any more scary television in future!

Instead, I encourage you to focus on the light, on your blessings, on the love, guidance and spiritual protection that is always with you. Remember the techniques I have given to you on protection and use them regularly, particularly if you are doing spiritual work or are in a situation where you feel vulnerable. Most importantly, please do not anticipate or worry about negative energies that may affect you. It is highly unlikely that they will, but the thinking about the possibility can bring about the belief they are there – and it is usually imagination!

In exceptional circumstances where there is genuine reason for anxiety, there are experts who can be called upon to investigate and clear dark energies.

GHOSTS AND EARTHBOUND SPIRITS

Ghosts do exist and I have seen them, but they are not to be concerned about except in exceptional circumstances. There are two types:

1. The first comes from **energetic memory**. In a place where there has been a traumatic event such as a battle or an untimely death, or where there has been an emotion or situation – peaceful, joyful, unhappy, whatever – which was particularly 'impressive', then the memory of what occurred can embed itself in the fabric of the place and certain sensitive individuals may see, hear or sense what occurred. There are stories of people seeing the re-enactment of famous historical events, but minor occurrences can be seen also. A Welsh farmer told me of a time when he was walking down an old bridleway near his home in the hills not far from where I live and found himself in the midst of a ghostly herd of cows which were being led to their milking shed by their owner. He heard them, felt them, saw them, smelled them

but there was nothing there physically. The 'green lane' as it was known had been used for that purpose for hundreds of years and the memory was literally impressed there.

No harm can come from such manifestations. Indeed, when they are tranquil energetic memories like the cows they are rather wonderful. Whether the memories are of sad or happy times they have nothing to do with you, and you are merely the observer.[6]

2. The second type of ghost is **a trapped soul**. I explained in Chapter Three on Life, Death and Reincarnation that every soul has a choice of exit points for when the soul will leave the body. No death is unplanned in spiritual terms and the most seemingly unexpected death will be the taking of an arranged exit point by that individual, though the personality, oblivious to the blueprint that has been drawn up before birth, will not be aware of the plan beforehand.

When you die, hopefully you will move to the astral or other plane without difficulty, ready to heal, learn and grow in the non-physical realms before reincarnating as a human being once again. There are some situations, however, when it doesn't work out that way and the soul either doesn't realise its body has died or it is unwilling – perhaps fearful – to move on. So, in both circumstances the entity lingers on, perhaps in the place it knew best or where the death of the body took place.

When this occurs the trapped soul will be puzzled as to why no one is taking any notice of it and it may take a long time or a reminder to tell it that it is no longer in body. In the film *Sixth Sense*, the hero who had died continued to work as a psychiatrist, believing he was alive, and the only person who could communicate with him and see him was a boy who could 'see dead people'.

When there has been a disaster like a train crash or a terrorist attack, the shock of the event may cause some chaos for a while with a number of souls unable to find their way back to the light. Most make it eventually, but some will need help to get there. There are certain spiritual practices known as 'Psychopomp' rituals which are specifically designed to help Earthbound souls leave the physical plane, but only if they wish to.

Psychopomp

Psychopomp is a shamanic tradition, though other people have their own ways of doing this work of releasing trapped souls. It is an act which is carried out with loving compassion to help souls return to the astral plane. It is not a form of exorcism, which deals with evicting what are seen to be evil or demonic entities.

For psychopomp practitioners it is essential to do the work with the greatest care and maximum spiritual protection: Earthbound spirits who were drug addicts or alcoholics, or who had mental problems, for example, or who died very angry, can be irrational and malevolent, and they can create serious problems for the unwary or careless would-be healer who moves into their world of shadows.

I know a number of shamans who specialise in helping Earthbound spirits to return home. They treat the work with the greatest seriousness and formality, with a set procedure and a group of spiritual helpers which includes their power animals (described in the section on Protection at the beginning of this book and also in Chapter Seven to come) and additional assistants, and the procedure, ritual if you like, is always the same, though unique to each practitioner.

Sometimes an Earthbound spirit refuses to leave the Earth plane they occupy. If so, nothing can be done until they are ready to move on.

HAUNTED HOUSES

When I was a little girl growing up in a large Victorian house in Kent I had some unpleasant experiences due to the activities of Great Uncle Cyril. Great Uncle Cyril was not mentioned within the family but my understanding was that he was discovered to be homosexual. One hundred years ago this was socially unacceptable and so the tricky problem about what to do with him was resolved by sending him to live in Australia where he lived quite an unhappy life.

When he died his soul returned to his beloved family home. He was angry at his banishment and of course everything was different from when he had left and so he was confused too. I think I occupied the same attic bedroom that had been his. Every night I lay in bed hearing heavy measured footsteps walking up the stairs and along the wooden corridor to my door and stop there right outside it. It was terrifying for a little girl and the manifestations worsened when, after a period of time, he entered the room and shook my mattress so hard that it was difficult to stay within the bed. I may have been tossed out altogether once or twice, but I always tried to blot out what was happening at the time because it was so horrible and so my memories of that time in my life, while vivid, are patchy. Fortunately, experiences such as this are very rare indeed.

Sadly for Great Uncle Cyril I didn't realise that he wanted help. This was a classic case where a professional in these matters could have freed him to return home and bring peace to the house. The house is now a hotel and much changed, so it may be that with the departure of his biological family from his family home he has found release.

Sometimes 'hauntings' occur because an Earthbound soul is asking for help to return to its spiritual home. This is different from the soul who has chosen to stay attached to the place where it lived when it was in body because it was so happy there. I have come across a number of houses where I have seen, for example, Ernest from Victorian times smoking his pipe contentedly by the fireside where he always sat and still does, or Mary picking flowers in her beloved garden. They stay because of their love for the place, or sometimes there is a purpose such as to protect it and the occupants. Ernest and Mary and their like will move on when they are ready and it is important not to force them away until that time comes, particularly when they are doing no harm.

Souls that know they are Earthbound and who don't know how to leave can be very disruptive in their attempt to gain attention and help, and often it is humans who are on the spiritual path who are affected: their light attracts the entity to them and it can be very persistent in its demands.

SUMMARY

Throughout this book I refer to and discuss the importance of choice for us all as part of our opportunity to experience, learn and grow. As part of this, there is a choice between the path of light and that of the dark as there is a choice in all things. Those who choose the latter are contributing to the cosmic dance just as are the Light-bearers and as such they are necessary players. Whatever *your* choice, it is fine, and perfect for you and the world. Just as it is possible for your inner demons to be sent packing, so it is possible, always, for all aspects of the dark which are negative or unhelpful to be brought into the light – if you so choose.

In this context, the exercise that follows will help you to see if there are negative elements around you in your life and to determine how potent they are and what to do about them.

Exercise 6: Identify people in your life who bring you negativity

I talked earlier in this chapter about how some people can make life difficult or uncomfortable for you because of their deliberate or unconscious negative attitude or behaviour towards you and how you can deal with this. It can help to identify who in your life comes into this category – and who brings light into your life also. That is what this exercise is all about.

It is not a meditation or spiritual practice as such, so it is not necessary to prepare your sacred space nor yourself beforehand as I usually ask you to do, unless you wish to. I suggest, nonetheless, that you put protection around yourself in whatever way you choose.

Please find a time and place where you will be undisturbed. When you are thinking about the time and place for it, please bear in mind that you may wish to do the exercise over several days. It is not one to be rushed.

When you are ready to begin, mentally connect with Spirit and the Brothers and Sisters of the Light. Ask them to help you with the work you are about to do.

- Take some paper – it may be your spiritual journal if you wish – and draw five columns on the page.

- At the top of the first column, write the heading 'Contacts'.

- At the top of the second column, write the heading 'People I trust absolutely always to treat me with love and kindness'.

- At the top of the third column, write the heading 'People who will love and help me, but only when it suits them'.

- At the top of the fourth column, write the heading 'People who have disappointed or let me down, and who dishonour me'.

- In the fifth column, put the heading 'Action to be taken'.

Now, in the first column write down the names of everyone who is in your life. The list will include family members, friends, work colleagues, certain acquaintances – anyone you talk to or communicate with regularly or from time to time. Please do not omit your partner, if you have one, or even your children. It is easy to assume they fit in column 2 but sometimes they turn out to be column 4 candidates.

Study each name carefully, see how you feel about them, what memories come up about your relationship with them. Then put a tick in the column that best describes their feelings towards you. You may find that column 2 has fewer names in it than the others, but it will be the most precious, for it will confirm to you those people in your life whom you can trust absolutely to love you unconditionally.

Completing column 5 will be interesting for you – deciding what to do. For some people no action will be necessary, but with some contacts you will wish, perhaps, to strengthen the relationship, in others you may wish to be less confiding; you may wish to distance yourself from some people, and others you may wish, gently, to remove from your life altogether. It is your choice, as always, but I suggest it is not helpful to you to have around you the negative energy of someone whom you cannot trust, who does not behave towards you with integrity or who saps your energy.

This exercise is intense but important. You may wish to work on it for an hour or so, then leave it for a while, perhaps until the next day, and then return to it with new names to add to your list or new thoughts and memories about those who are already there.

Chapter Six
The Rays

Our connection to the divine gives rise to many wonders, one of which is the mystery of the seven great Rays which guide our lives.[1] These Rays, which emanate from the Source of all that is, or God if you wish, are important because they have a tremendous influence on your personality, soul and spirit, and every aspect of your being is at all times affected by one or all of the Rays directly or indirectly.

Alice Bailey has written extensively on the Rays. Her analysis, while excellent and unsurpassed, is complex and can be challenging for the modern reader to grasp. My intention in writing this chapter is to make it as easy as possible for you to appreciate what they are, why they matter, and their importance for you.

A simple way to understand the Rays is to begin by seeing God, the Source, as an immense ball of light encompassing everything so that, in effect, light is everywhere. Now see that ball of white light as being divided into seven sections, each section with its own colour and attributes, representing an aspect, a quality of God. Putting them together they encompass the totality of God. Because you are so strongly influenced by the Rays in every aspect of your life, as you will see in this chapter, it is another way of saying that the totality of God in every aspect is all around and within you.

These Rays are great bands of light energy which stream down upon the Earth, influencing everything on their path – the cosmos, the solar system, the planets, Earth, nations and races, groups of people and individuals. By the time the Rays reach you they will have filtered through many levels – cosmic, cyclical, planetary and human – absorbing a subtle impression of the energy of the different levels they have passed through to reach you and serving also to connect you to those levels.

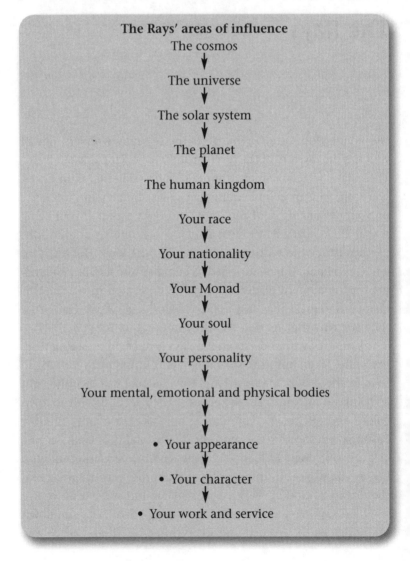

The Rays' areas of influence

The cosmos
↓
The universe
↓
The solar system
↓
The planet
↓
The human kingdom
↓
Your race
↓
Your nationality
↓
Your Monad
↓
Your soul
↓
Your personality
↓
Your mental, emotional and physical bodies
↓
↓
• Your appearance
↓
• Your character
↓
• Your work and service

The Rays are linked to the colours of the rainbow and the chakras and have distinct characteristics from each other, which I will describe in detail shortly. Just as each Ray impacts on you differently to someone else, so the Rays also impact on the planets in the solar system differently one from another.

You yourself have a carefully defined Ray pattern which is unique to you and which was defined in the prebirth planning that I talked about in Chapter Three. The Lords of Karma will have taken into account your karmic lessons, your stage of spiritual evolution and your soul's purpose in constructing your Ray pattern, and that pattern will be different with each new incarnation to take into account what you need to learn and achieve in your new life.

Let's look at the Rays in more detail and see how they apply to you.

THE SEVEN RAYS DEFINED

There are three main, or major Rays, esoterically known as the Rays of Aspect, and four further sub-Rays known as the Rays of Attribute or Characteristic.

The major Rays

1. Ray of Will, Power and Intent (colour: red)
2. Ray of Love and Wisdom (colour: blue)
3. Ray of Active Intelligence (or Philosophy and Political Activism) (colour: yellow)

The Rays of attribute or characteristic

4. Ray of Harmony through Conflict, and the Arts (colour: green)
5. Ray of Concrete Knowledge, Science and the Intellect (colour: orange)
6. Ray of Devotion and Idealism (colour: indigo)
7. Ray of Ceremonial Magic and Order (colour: violet)

There are further Rays beyond the seven listed here, but these are the ones which influence you and the planet particularly.

HOW THE RAYS IMPACT ON YOU

I have explained in other chapters how the purpose of your life journey is to experience everything there is about being human, and that each lifetime presents the opportunities to learn about certain aspects of being in body, to overcome weaknesses or short-comings you may have and to enhance your gifts. The Rays are a crucially important part of this process.

In each lifetime every aspect of you will be dominated by one or other of the Rays, whether it is that which is spirit, soul, personality, your physical body, your emotions or how your mind works. Each Ray has its own quality to help you learn and grow, particularly where it influences your mind, emotions and physicality, and your personality – your strengths and frailties. As you can see, therefore, the Rays are closely connected to the Earth lessons that are part of the soul journey described in Chapter Four.

During your entire human experience through all your incarnations it is necessary to experience all the Rays, in all the different parts of you, and to assimilate them as strengths. This is another way of saying that you cannot reach and pass the seventh level of learning, when you no longer need to reincarnate back on Earth, until the quality of every Ray has been experienced by you in its most perfect form at every level within you. This means, for example, that your physical body will have had lifetimes of being strong, lanky, graceful, refined, awkward or compact. Charts that follow will show you the different qualities applicable to each Ray and how they impact on your emotions, mind, personality and so on both as negatives (your inner demons) and as strengths.

The exception to this rule of Ray-experiencing concerns your Monad, that part of you which is Spirit and so constant in its perfection. Because it is perfect, the Ray which governs your Monad is always, throughout your soul journey, one of the three major Rays that concern power, loving wisdom and the intellect.

Similarly, the Ray which influences your soul rarely changes but stays the same for a complete Earth cycle of experience lasting possibly thousands of years. It can be governed by any one of the seven Rays, but when the third initiatory test has taken place and your soul is in the driving seat at last, the soul *must* move to be governed by one of the three major Rays if it is not doing so already. This can happen in the course of a particular lifetime and may result in the person seeming to change character or behaviour suddenly and unexpectedly.

The Ray affecting your personality will change from lifetime to lifetime, as will the Rays influencing your appearance, emotions, creativity, mental capacity, strengths and weaknesses, relation-ships and career. Each Ray can be used positively and negatively so that, for example, a first Ray temperament can show strength and courage, or aggression and bullying. Part of your challenge is to see when you are using a Ray negatively and then to transform it to being a positive.

WHY DO YOU NEED TO KNOW YOUR RAY PATTERN?

The Rays can seem quite complicated because the concept of unseen energies influencing who and how we are so enormously can be strange if you have not come across it before. Indeed some people ask why they need to know about the Rays. What good will it do? In fact, if you know what the different Rays are that govern your body and your life in a particular lifetime, then it can assist you to:

- See what your lessons are for that lifetime, the potential weak-nesses to be aware of and what to aim for in every area of your life.

- Understand which relationships will work and which will not. If you find yourself in a friendship, work situation or romantic partnership with someone whose Ray profile is very different from yours, you will see more clearly their attitudes and priorities and how they differ from yours and be able to make allowances.

Because the Rays impact on you so very strongly, you will be attracted to or feel an affinity with those people who share the same Ray pattern to a certain degree. The expression 'on the same wavelength' refers, in fact, to having, somewhere in your make-up, Ray similarities. Where someone has a totally different Ray make-up from you, then it is likely you will have nothing in common with them and will not wish to be in their company. Two people with the same soul Ray will become great friends because the one will recognise himself or herself in the other. When the personality Ray is also the same there is an unbreakable link and a perfect marriage or friendship is formed. However, people with the same personality Ray only and a different soul Ray will have brief, sudden relationships which are soon over.

- If doctors and psychologists could see and address our Ray make-up and any imbalances there instead of seeing us just as 'bodies' it would transform the health and well-being of humanity, for they would be able to recognise our physical, mental, emotional, even spiritual weaknesses, see where they are and know what to do and advise to strengthen them.

A chart to assist you to identify your Ray make-up is given later in this chapter. First, let's consider the meaning of each Ray in broad terms.

THE MEANING OF THE RAYS

So, each Ray has a specific quality that can be used as a strength or as a weakness to be overcome. It may help to consider what the positive and negative attributes of each Ray are:

Ray 1: Will, Power, and Intent[2]

Strengths	Weaknesses
Strength of will	Selfishness and self-centredness
Dynamic power	Excessive pride
Power to bring projects or people together	Being unsociable, keeping yourself apart
Strong sense of purpose	Arrogance
Ability to identify and eliminate what is unhelpful or damaging	Wilfulness
Strong intention and focus	Hunger for power
Power to encourage and preserve integrity	Domination
Power to lead	Destructiveness
Power to direct	Anger and violence
Power to govern	Unrelenting ambition
Fearlessness	Hardness and cruelty
Power to initiate	Control and suppression
Detachment, or the power to detach	Inhibition
Wisdom to establish, uphold or enforce the law	Impatience
Strength and courage	Obstinacy
Independence	
Power to liberate	
Keen understanding of principles and priorities	
Truthfulness arising from absolute fearlessness	
Power to consolidate, unify and streamline	
Generosity	

Ray 2: Love and Wisdom[3]

Strengths	Weaknesses
Loving wisdom	Fearfulness
Charm and charisma	Self-pity
Power to understand through love	Over-sensitivity and vulnerability
Empathy, sympathy and compassion	Tendency towards an inferiority complex
Discerning sensitivity towards others	Over-attachment
Open-mindedness and persuasibility	Over-protectiveness, over guarding
Love of pure truth	Love of being loved
Intuitive love	Timid
Clear perception and intelligence	Over-absorption in study
Concern for group inclusiveness and agreement	Tendency to be a 'people-pleaser'
Power to teach and illumine	Reluctance to take action when it is called for
Patience	Coldness and indifference to others
Tact	Contempt for mental limitations in others
Serenity	
Faithfulness	
Tolerance	
Power to help people learn and grow	
Power to heal through love	

Ray 3: Active Intelligence[4]

Strengths	Weaknesses
Capacity for philosophical and intellectual thinking	Intellectual pride
Capacity to hypothesise and ponder	Excessive criticism
Understanding that knowledge is not absolute, but is relative	Vague and overly complex thought and expression of thought
Wide views on all abstract questions	Perplexity and confusion
Capacity for rigorous analysis and reasoning: an acute and powerful intellect	Absent-mindedness
Great mental creativity	Excessive thinking without practical action
Ability to adjust and change ideas for the sake of accuracy in thought	Inaccuracy in practical detail; carelessness
Power to understand and explain complex patterns and trends in ideas and theories	Being manipulative and calculating
Great mental activity and agility	Taking advantage of a situation at others' expense
Skilful communication; the power to be vocal and express complex ideas in words, simply	Deviousness, deceitfulness, untruth
Good with languages	Unreliable
Power to understand and develop theories about the Divine Plan for Earth and beyond	Greed for money and objects
Power to influence people and concepts	Hyperactivity, restlessness, lots of wasted activity without result
Ability to plan for the long and the short term	Disorder and chaos
Great activity and adaptability	Tendency to be 'spread too thin', poor time-management
Ability to understand economy and be economical	Constant preoccupation and 'busyness'
Facility for understanding and handling money; philanthropy and public-spiritedness	
Managerial and business abilities	

Ray 4: Harmony through Conflict[5]

Strengths	Weaknesses
Facility for bringing harmony out of conflict	Embroiled in constant conflict and turmoil (inner and outer)
Capacity to grow spiritually and psychologically through constant struggle and crisis	Self-absorption in suffering, lack of confidence and composure
Capacity to reconcile	Worry and agitation
Facility for bringing dissonant parts together into unity	Excessive moodiness
Facility for compromise, mediation and bridging	Melodramatic tendencies, and tendency to exaggeration
Capacity for creating beauty out of what was inharmonious	Emotional instability, impracticality and carelessness with money
Love of beauty and the capacity to create or express it	Unstable activity patterns; spasmodic action
Clear and sensitive perception of people and situations	Unpredictability and unreliability
Strong imagination and intuition	Wanting to argue and fight for the sake of it without knowing why
Love of colour	Ambivalence, indecisiveness and vacillation
Strong sense of drama	Over-eagerness for compromise
Ability to amuse, delight and entertain	Moral cowardice
Musicality	Lack of self-control, self-indulgence
Literary abilities via creative imagination	Laziness and procrastination
Spontaneity and improvisation	
Fighting spirit	
Ability to make peace	

Ray 5: Concrete Knowledge, Science and the Intellect[6]

Strengths	Weaknesses
Capacity to think and act scientifically	An unbalanced focus on mental activity to the detriment of the emotions and the soul
Keen and focused intellect, strong mental concentration	Excessive analysis, rationalisation and use of logic
Power to define thoughts and concepts	Rejection of all non-material possibilities, such as spirituality or theology, in favour of what is tangible and demonstrable
Power to create clear and well-articulated ideas	Excessive doubt and scepticism; irreverence
Facility for mathematical calculation	Lack of intuitive sensitivity
Highly developed powers of analysis and discrimination	Excessive objectivity
Detached objectivity	Rigid and set thought patterns
Accuracy and precision in thought and action	Narrowness and prejudice
Acquisition of knowledge and the mastery of factual detail	Harsh criticism
Power to discover through investigation and research	Lack of emotional responsiveness and charisma; social awkwardness
Power to verify through experimentation; the discrimination of truth from error	
Ability to create and construct ideas, objects, machines, technologies	
Practical inventiveness	
Technical expertise	
Common sense and the rejection of 'non-sense'	

Ray 6: Devotion and Abstract Idealism[7]

Strengths	Weaknesses
Spiritual idealism and vision	Rigid idealism, leading to blindness to new ideas or opportunities
Power to detach from the world of materialism	Meaningless devotion; ill-considered loyalty
Intense spiritual devotion	Blind faith
Willingness to sacrifice your life for your beliefs	Doing everything to excess
Unshakeable faith and undimmed optimism	Unvarying single-mindedness, ultra-narrow focus; rigidity of thought, mania
Total single-mindedness, focused on achieving the goal or intention	Fanaticism, uncontrolled intensity and action
Utter loyalty and adherence	Tendency to excessive display of emotion
Earnestness and sincerity	Selfish and jealous love; dependency; over-dependency on others
Profound humility	Habit of being easily led, particularly by their 'spiritual betters'; overly deferential
Receptivity to spiritual guidance	Superstition and gullibility; lack of realism
Unflagging persistence	Low self-esteem; masochism; the martyr-complex
Power to arouse, inspire and persuade	Unnatural suppression of instinct and intuition
Ability to achieve ecstasy and rapture	Idealistic impracticality
Purity, goodness, sainthood	

Ray 7: Order and Ceremonial Magic[8]

Strengths	Weaknesses
Power to create order out of chaos	Rigid orderliness, fear of change, dislike of spontaneity
Practicality and common sense	Over-concern with and automatic acceptance of traditional rules, regulations and the 'dead letter' of the law
Power to plan and organise	Blind and rigid focus on old practices and routines
Practical and spiritual ability to devise routines, rituals or ceremonies	Dependency and insistence on doing things as they have always been done without thinking about why, and if there is a better way
Power as a magician	Materialism; concern with the world of physical objects and practices only
Power to work with the nature spirits and forces of nature	Intolerance of individuality; lack of originality
Organisational creativity and expertise	Excessive conformity (or non-conformity); intolerance of anything new (or old)
Power to manage detail	Excessive perfectionism; judgemental of those who do not measure up to the high standards expected
Keen sense of rhythm and timing, a good understanding of the concept and use of the Cycles of Time and Space for people and projects	Bigotry and narrow-mindedness
Power to co-ordinate groups	Superficial judgement based upon appearances
Power to understand, create and implement the law through an altruistic desire for practical action	Use of spiritual ritual and processes for personal gain (black magic)
Understanding of how ideas and objects fit together, and the sequences, to create what is needed	Misuse of sexual energy for physical pleasure or for power over others

Strengths	Weaknesses
Power to bring about renewal and transformation	Addiction to occult phenomena; spiritualism; a demanding of demonstrable proof of the existence of Spirit without accepting your personal responsibility for your soul journey
Power to bring projects, people and ideas together in a practical sense	Fear of insecurity

THE RAY LORDS

Each Ray is headed up by a 'Ray Lord' who epitomises the strengths of that Ray and oversees its work and impact. So, Lord Kuthumi, who is the Master in charge of Ray 2 (which is to do with Love and Wisdom) has the second Ray as His Monadic Ray and has responsibility for all the spiritual teachers and healers on Earth who are working to help to generate spiritual understanding and love among humanity.

Each of us, you see, is connected to one of the Ray Lords according to our Monadic Ray, which never changes. If you remember, the Ray which governs your Monad is always either Ray 1, 2 or 3 (the three major Rays, as discussed above) because the Monad is pure spirit and therefore always perfect.

If you wish to strengthen a particular Ray quality in yourself, it can be very helpful to ask to go, in your meditation, to meet the Lord of that particular Ray and ask Him for assistance.

THE RAYS AND THE CHAKRAS

Each chakra is governed by a Ray, wherever it is, whether it is a chakra within you and everyone else, or one which exists in a life beyond you, such as within planet Earth herself. The following chart shows the relationship between the chakras and the Rays and also how the Rays and chakras correlate with the seven stages, or tests, of the soul's journey which I described in Chapter Four.

Chakra	Ray	Ray Number	Stage of Soul Learning
7. Crown centre (violet)	Ray of Will and Power (red)	First	Lesson 7 (Merger – with God)
6. Third eye (indigo)	Ray of Concrete Knowledge, Science and the Intellect (orange)	Fifth	Lesson 6 (Decision — ascension)
5. Throat centre (sky blue)	Ray of Active Intelligence (yellow)	Third	Lesson 5 (Revelation – start of ascension process)
4.Heart centre (pink or green)	Ray of Love and Wisdom (blue)	Second	Lesson 4 (Suffering, or renunciation – soul merger with the Monad)
3.Solar plexus (yellow)	Ray of Devotion and Idealism (indigo)	Sixth	
2. Sacral centre (orange)	Ray of Ceremonial Magic and Order (violet)	Seventh	Lesson 3 (Mental control)
1. Root chakra (red)	Ray of Harmony through Conflict and the Arts (green or pink)	Fourth	Lesson 2 (Emotional control)
			Lesson 1 (Physical control)

If you study the chart with care, you will notice that the colour associated with each chakra differs from the colour of its corresponding Ray. If you wish to strengthen the qualities within you that are to do with a particular soul lesson and its Ray, then to work with the colour both of that Ray and the associated chakra will help tremendously. For example, if you are undergoing the fourth level of soul learning, to do with suffering as part of the merger of your soul with your Monad, then you may wish to bring the colours that are pink, or green, and blue into your life, perhaps through clothing, through flowers around you, even the decor in your home.

HOW TO IDENTIFY YOUR RAY PROFILE

Having spent so much time considering the importance of the Rays and what they mean to you and your journey through life, the question you may be asking now is, how do I find out what my Rays are?

There are a number of ways:

- You may wish to start by studying the chart that follows. It looks at the different Ray characteristics for the personality, mental, emotional and physical aspects of being human, also the soul. If you look at each column and reflect upon which category feels to you to be most like you it will help you identify your Rays. Please remember that your Ray profile for each category may not, necessarily, have one Ray exclusively dominant over another. It may be that you have aspects of a couple of Rays influencing your mental processes, for example, so try and see which characteristic is strongest for you in each category.

- Michael D. Robbins, author of the excellent *Tapestry of the Gods* and founder of the Seven Ray Institute in the United States, has made a life-long and erudite study of Alice Bailey's work on the Rays and has devised a Personal Identity Profile to help you understand your Ray structure. It is a detailed self-assessment inventory/questionnaire which, on completion, is analysed by the Seven Ray Institute to produce your Ray make-up. Details of the Institute are given in the Resources section.

- Some people have used hypnotherapy, past life regression and meditation to gain guidance about their Rays. Please see the Exercise given at the end of this chapter.

Summary of the Ray types by soul, personality, mental, emotional and physical qualities[9]

Ray	Soul qualities	Personality qualities	Mental qualities	Emotional qualities	Physical qualities
1	Dynamic charge of spiritual will and power.	Fortitude, assurance, firmness, independence. Also, proud, dominating, self-centred, selfish.	Firmness in thought and opinion. A mind that is dominating, 'impressive', decisive, for principles not details, concentrated, critical, active, independent, detached, realistic, occult.	Emotional power, suppression, unresponsiveness, compulsion; hidden tenseness and anxiety, temper and destructive emotion, fear of emotional attachment, emotional isolation.	Physically powerful, intense physical energy, stiff, awkward or sudden movements, lanky but strong, dislike of being touched, strong head emphasis.
2	Glowing suffusion of loving wisdom.	Able to express love wisely, understand people deeply; patient, tactful, compassionate. Also timid, fearful, too tolerant, too attached to own comforts, need to be liked.	A mind that is abstract, all-absorbing, receptive, passive, comprehensive and inclusive, synthesising, non-critical, clear, still, pondering, detailed, illuminated.	Loving, calm, gentle, serene, patient, empathetic, compassionate, protective, altruistic, sensitive, can be overwhelmed.	Soft, sensitive, inactive – love of ease and idleness, magnetic, non-assertive, likes to be touched, fear of being hurt physically, empathetic – strong heart emphasis.

Ray	Soul qualities	Personality qualities	Mental qualities	Emotional qualities	Physical qualities
3	Inflow of creative, versatile, active and acute intelligence reflecting the Divine plan.	Resourceful, adaptable, creatively intelligent. Self-reliant, strategic. Also, an exaggerated sense of personal intelligence, lives by intellect not love.	An active, reasoning, analytical and deductive mind, also manipulative, critical, creative, abstract, calculating, strategic, versatile, eclectic and circuitous.	Psychic, autonomous, disordered, chaotic, materialistic, desire-driven.	Very active, a 'busy' body, physical resilience and endurance, muscular frame, strong pain threshold, rapid brain activity, strong throat emphasis.
4	Irresistible inner urge to bring harmony and beauty out of conflict and chaos.	Ability to create peace and beauty of relationship by harmonising conflicts and resolving dissonances. Also, lack of self-control, unreliable, unstable, vacillating, inconsistent, need to reduce their turbulence and learn how to express divine love through beauty and balance.	A mind that is mediating, reconciling, unifying, balancing, reasoning, receptive, intuitive, imaginative, expressive, dramatic, exaggerative, quick, paradoxical or conflicted.	Constant emotional struggle and conflict, ambivalence, moodiness, emotional longing and need for peace and beauty, strong emotional and intuitive connection.	Etheric ebbs and flows. Physical agitation, 'paralysis' of activity, balanced, refined, graceful movement, beauty of form, well proportioned, responsive to beauty in the environment, brain very responsive to intuition and holistic thought, strong third eye activity.

Ray	Soul qualities	Personality qualities	Mental qualities	Emotional qualities	Physical qualities
5	Unremitting urge to penetrate the veils of matter and form until their secret causes are revealed and their natures exactly disclosed.	Ability to gain exact knowledge through focused, concentrated thinking and scientific experimentation. Also, too narrow a focus on their own mental and technical interests, intellectual mistrust of the non-scientific and what they cannot prove.	A scientific mind and one that is precise, accurate, focused, analytical, literal, lucid, clinical, objective, detached, unbiased, probing, technical, mathematical, critical, unimaginative.	Flat, colourless, unemotional, rational, mind-dominated, detached.	Hard, compact, somewhat rigid, awkward, isolating, responsive to the concrete mind, strong brow activity – but differing from the Fourth Ray person.
6	Unrelenting urge to find and follow someone (or something) to which total devotion can be given.	Ability to devote to a person or cause with intense focus and to live true to the highest ideals. Also, can be fanatical, unreasonable, rigid, narrow, emotional, extreme. Obsessively preoccupied with the focus of desire.	A highly focused mind, repetitive thought content, dogmatic, evangelical, inflexible, passive, ideologically limited.	Emotional dependency, lack of control, selfish loving, emotional intensity and persistence, fanatical, intense, delusional, obsessive.	Loose muscle tone, tendency to accumulate fluids, strong emphasis on the emotions. Can be addictive, physical tenacity and persistence, a fiery physical nature.

Ray	Soul qualities	Personality qualities	Mental qualities	Emotional qualities	Physical qualities
7	The urge to manifest divine ideas in perfect form.	Able to demonstrate efficient organisational or administrative prowess, as well as courteous team spirit. Also, resistant to change, too locked in routine, tradition and personal routines.	An organising, sorting mind, constructive when mentally creating, detailed, consistent, excellent memory, formality of expression, predictable, habit-driven, inflexible, conforming to the rules, likes mantras and affirmations.	A disciplined and appropriate emotional response, predictable, influenced by the rhythms of the physical body and the material world. Inclined towards mediumship and spiritualism.	Refined and delicate, graceful, etheric sensitivity, responsive to rhythmic cycles, body easily trained, attentive to physical order in the environment, well grounded, inclined to use the hands for healing and practical activities.

Exercise 7: Meditation to help identify your Ray(s)

- Prepare for meditation in the normal way. Wherever you are, imagine that you are in your home and that no one else is there.

- Take three deep breaths and focus on your breathing for a few moments.

- Remind yourself that it is your intention to identify one or more of your Rays.

- As you sit in your silence, ponder on the Rays for a moment. Think about what they represent and see if any particular Ray comes to your mind. If it does, then it will have a connection for you and you may wish to make a mental note of it and how you feel about it.

- You hear a knock on the door of your home. Get up and open the door. Outside, you see an angel, your Guardian Angel who has manifested to assist you. Greet your Angel in the way you wish.

- Ask your Angel to give you the information about your Rays that is appropriate for you to have at this time.

- The Angel beckons you out of your home and leads you to a small building with an open door. As you go in, you see you are in an art gallery with seven paintings hanging around the room, each one numbered and named.

- The Angel takes you to a particular painting. Look at the number and see what it is called. It may say 'soul', or 'mind' or 'personality' or 'emotions' or 'body'. You are being shown an aspect of you and the number is the Ray which is governing it. Look at the picture itself and see what it is showing you about the nature of the Ray and how it applies to you.

- Ask your Angel if there is another painting for you to look at. If there is, repeat the exercise and do so as long as the Angel has a painting for you to look at.

- Make a mental note of what you have learnt. Then allow your Angel to lead you from the gallery and take you back to your home. Thank your Angel.

- When you are ready, close down your chakras, put protection around yourself and return to your everyday reality.

- Finally, write down what you have seen, experienced and learned in your spiritual journal.

Chapter Seven

Our Spiritual Helpers

While it may seem sometimes as if your journey through your Earth lessons and experiences is a lonely struggle, this is a false perception that comes from being unaware of or not trusting your spiritual connections. The reality is very different.

We have already looked at how many cosmic beings are involved in working with you before you are born to create the perfect circumstances for your next life, such as the Lords of Karma and your own spiritual team. That support is available throughout this and every lifetime, but the degree of support you are given depends upon how far you ask for help and how evolved you are as a soul. It is only those people whose souls have awakened who are starting to think about other people rather than their own physical needs, and who, therefore, have a spiritual mission, who have a team of spirit guides working with them. Your team has been put together very carefully indeed to help you achieve that mission – if you are willing to let them and if you remember to ask for their help.

THE IMPORTANCE OF ASKING FOR HELP

As you know by now, however much guidance from higher realms is available to you, nonetheless it is the choices that *you* make that determine what happens in your life and how far you will achieve your mission. Nothing can be imposed on you by some-one else, in human terms, unless you choose it to occur or you allow it to be so. In the same way it is a spiritual law that your non-physical helpers cannot give you their assistance directly unless you ask for it.

I have come across many people who complain that they cannot connect with their guides and that Spirit does nothing to help them. They do not realise that there is a great team of beings of light standing by and watching helplessly and sadly as their protégé insists on going it alone. All they can do is send signposts and messages to them indirectly in the hope that he or she will receive them somehow.

The situation is a little like a stay in a five-star hotel that you have won in a major competition. You come into the foyer, sit down on the smallest chair you can find and take out a supermar-ket sandwich and bottle of water from your bag. You eat it, watching, with some envy, all the affluent guests come and go before you before finding a hard pillow and sleeping uncomfort-ably in the same chair all night. You have forgotten that there is a chambermaid waiting to welcome you to your room, which is filled with flowers, a well-stocked mini-bar and all comforts, that there are chefs and waiters in the kitchens and dining room long-ing to prepare a feast for the star guest – you. All you have to do is to ask for the prize which you have earned: unless you do you will receive little if anything of what is available to you, which is yours by right. So it is with the world of Spirit. If you do not ask for their help your assistants can do little for you and you truly are on your own in this world.

If you are going to ask for their help, it helps to have an idea of who is out there waiting to support and work with you, to make your connection with them more personal. Before looking at some of the ways you can do this, I would like to describe the dif-ferent groups of helpers that we souls here on Earth have to call upon.

THE SPIRITUAL SUPPORT TEAMS

Relatives who have died

I dealt earlier with the subject of what happens when you die and where you go. Your destination, as you will remember, is usually the astral plane and the lower levels where most of us go when we die are close to the physical reality of Earth. So, relatives and friends who have died are close to you also, and because they loved you in their previous life, so that love and wish to help continues. Sometimes they will make their presence felt to you quite unexpectedly and you will feel the familiarity of their energy near you and know they are visiting. You may have dreams about them and when they are very vivid it is likely they are real and that you were indeed together while your soul was on its travels during your sleep state.

Mary is a friend and client of mine. Some years ago her father died, but because her parents had divorced when she was young and he lived abroad from then on, while sorry, she was not greatly upset by his passing. He had been a difficult man while he was alive and had shown no interest in or affection for his children, and so she was surprised one night to have a strong dream in which she was sitting on a chair looking at an enormous book placed on a stand in front of her. The book was open and she saw clearly her father standing by it with a long teacher's pointer moving across the page – he was talking to her, but also clearly teaching her from the tome. It was a little like something out of Harry Potter, except this took place before Harry came to life on page and screen.

She asked me to explain what the dream meant. I checked with my guides and discovered that her father felt guilty for neglecting her when he was alive and had determined, as part of his learning on the astral plane, where he was living, to help her as best he could, which included helping her spiritual education.

Your relatives on the higher planes who loved you when they were with you in physical body will do all they can for you and try to guide you as they did when they were alive. If you are sensitive you may feel their energy, sense a perfume associated with them, you may even see them or hear their voice. You may come across a photograph or other reminder of them unexpectedly and this may indicate they are with you and wish you to know it. It can be very comforting to be aware of their presence, particularly if you are grieving for them.

There are people who specialise in helping you to connect with loved ones who have passed on. A good medium can see, hear and sense those who are around you, and their ability to describe with accuracy what they look like and to communicate messages from them to you can be a wonderful confirmation that they are still alive even if you cannot see them. This applies to pets as well as people – and pets can have excellent advice for their 'owners'!

Always remember that the characteristics and prejudices your friends or relatives had when they were alive are still with them on the astral plane. So, if someone was disapproving about your way of life before they died, the same message may come through! You don't become a saint just because you have died. You are just the same, except that you don't have a body.

A well-known medium whom I will call Alfred told me a story about his mother, who had died some years before. His mother had been very house proud and had berated her son continually for, as she saw it, his untidy habits. On the night she died she came to him. He expected a loving and reassuring message from her but instead, to his amusement, all she came to say was, 'Alfred, you are living in a pigsty. When are you going to learn to use a duster?'

Your spirit guides

The meticulous planning that lies behind each of your many life-times, to ensure that your mission for your new journey on the Earth plane has the greatest chance of success, includes arranging for the perfect support team to be in place to assist you behind the scenes. You are part of that team: you happen to be the one soul within the group that is incarnate at this time like so many times before, but every team member has a vital part to play to achieve the group mission.

It is rather like a concert for a rock star, where there is the 'star' on stage but who cannot achieve a fantastic performance without the producer, the orchestra, the make-up ladies, the costumier, the set-designer, the ticket organiser, the canteen staff and so on. You are the star of your particular performance, the one who is visible now, but there are many great souls who are helping you – if you are willing – behind the scenes. Next time it may be another 'member' of the team who is in the limelight on Earth, while you are supporting them in a particular way from the non-physical realms.

Each guide, then, has a role and function specific to the needs of the mission and you. One guide may be a gatekeeper, assisting doors to open and the right contacts to be made. Another may be there to guide you to the tools that will help your work. Another may work with your Guardian Angel, or be your Guardian Angel to ensure your protection, while yet another will have a responsi-bility to do with ensuring your physical well-being.

You are unlikely to be aware of all the many guides who are working for you, and indeed a lot of people have no idea they have a team of spirit guides at all. It is a great sadness to the team when this occurs.

The guides who are most familiar to you are those souls who are working most closely with you, to teach you the strengths and les-sons you need at a particular period of your Earth journey. They may be with you for some years or just months.

My first experience of meeting one of my guides was soon after my spiritual awakening. I decided to do a meditation one afternoon in my home and as I started to return from it back to reality I opened my eyes and saw, sitting in a small chair at the far end of the room, a man dressed as a harlequin looking out of the window into the garden – he seemed a bit bored, as if he were waiting for me to come back. As I looked at him in some shock, he turned round swiftly to look at me and vanished. He looked made of flesh and blood, totally real, and I can picture him clearly to this day. The harlequin, my guide, showed himself to me as a visible reminder to me to have fun, joy and humour in my life – that was his job. He worked with me closely for some time until I learnt his teaching and was able to move on.

Usually you will have two or three key guides helping you learn and grow at any one time. Because they are so close to you, you can, with practice, learn to communicate with them and feel their presence around you. They may be family members who are in the spirit world, members of your soul group, people you have known in past incarnations or even animals. Every guide is an evolved soul who has earned the right to do this important work. Your guides work exclusively with you and for you, no one else and you may find some of the same guides assisting you through a number of different incarnations. Other guides are with you during a particular incarnation only.

Because your guides are with you to help you develop the qualities you need, as you progress and move on to another level of learning there will be a changeover, rather like the Changing of the Guard, and another guide from the team who has been waiting for this moment will come forward with the appropriate characteristics to help you. No member of the team will leave you during your mission on Earth and a guide whose job is done will retreat to the sidelines, but will still be supporting and assisting you.

In Chapter Four I discussed the initiations which are part of the soul's journey, including the fourth initiation of the Crucifixion when the soul is subsumed into the Monad. It is known as 'the dark night of the soul' and can be a time of great sorrow and anguish. At this point of your soul development your guides appear to leave you for a period of time and you may experience great loneliness, which is an important part of this particular lesson. In fact they have merely retreated. They are always close enough to come to your help if it is necessary.

It may be, if you have reached a certain level of soul evolution, that when you leave this life you will become a guide to a soul who is incarnating just as a member of your spiritual team is a guide to you now.

Your Master

Your different spirit guides work with you directly for lifetime after lifetime, and for very many people this is the highest form of spiritual support you will receive until your soul journey is quite advanced.

However, you have also another highly evolved spiritual being to which you are affiliated and this is your Master. Your Master (and the energy may be feminine or masculine) is rather like the Head of a large school or university. When you first join the institution you are there along with hundreds of others and are likely to be pretty indistinguishable from your peers. The Head may not notice you or be much interested in you until you begin to progress and to show some talent. The Head starts to keep an eye on your progress and then, as you become quite senior and your talent become distinguished or at least promising, the Head will take a direct hand in your education and you will come to know and be mentored by Him or Her personally.

Your Master will only become aware of you when your soul has activated and then it will be a remote interest. Periodically He or She will receive reports on your progress but there will be no contact. As you advance spiritually, lifetime after lifetime, so your Master becomes more involved with you directly. At first there will be sporadic contact between you and this will increase until you are being called to attend spiritual seminars and tutorials with Him or Her on a regular basis, when you are worthy of the attention.

This and other training takes place when you are asleep or in meditation, the time when the soul is free to leave your body and travel. As you progress spiritually, so your soul journeys to the Halls of Wisdom and Learning while you sleep, to learn from the Masters and other great teachers. This can explain why you may wake up feeling very tired despite having had a full night's sleep, or why you have strong dreams sometimes.

Like the university Head, your Master has responsibility for a number of individuals, not just you. If He or She is particularly senior, such as one of the Ray Lords, or has one of the great positions of state within the spiritual hierarchy, He or She will have junior Masters to assist Their work and the supervision of younger souls. All Masters, however evolved they may be, are working, learning and expanding on their path just as you are. Eventually They will move on to other duties, which brings opportunities for promotion for the younger Masters and eventually for you too.

So, unlike your guides who are concerned solely with you, your Master has a number of souls under supervision and you will know many of them for they are part of your soul group.

The reason for your connection with a particular Master or group of Masters is not random. Often it is because you are all working on a particular Ray or, if you are a very advanced initiate it may be because you are on the same initiatory path. Sometimes you may find you are working for two Masters: the Master who has responsibility for your soul journey over many lifetimes and in between lives and you may be seconded also to work alongside another Master for some specific work in a particular lifetime.

Masters have other roles besides assisting us on our soul

journey. Some work in other parts of the universe, others are working specifically to assist the evolution of the planet. Many have had lives on Earth also, but have reached such a high level of light they have completed all the initiations possible for the Earthly cycle and are on a much higher path.

One day you will be a Master with your own role and group of soul students in your own right, particularly if you choose to continue working to assist humanity after you have passed the seventh initiation. For most of us, this is a long way ahead!

As you become more advanced as a soul, so you will have the ability to connect with all the great Masters, each of whom represents a particular unique quality, for them to assist you if you feel the need for it.

Remember, our helpers in spirit cannot assist us until or unless we ask for it. This applies to our Masters also.

The angelic realms

Angels play an important part in your life and they are all around you. They occupy their own dimension which is the angelic realm. Angels are androgynous and they have distinct characteristics ranging from gentle to austere. They are powerful, determined and have a sense of purpose that is unflinching. Angels do not have free will to make choices as humanity on Earth has.

There are different angels for different situations in your life. There are angels who help to build your body and personality before a new incarnation begins – this is one of the reasons why they are known as the builders. Everything that exists on Earth has been created by angels.

Your Guardian Angel accompanies you through every lifetime and works exclusively with you, no one else. It is tremendously beneficial to get to know your own angel, to feel its energy and presence always around you. Even though, like your guides, your personal angel does not have a tangible body, nonetheless it can perform physical miracles in order to protect and care for you. I know this from personal experience.

One day, when I was working in Westminster, London, I went out in my lunch hour to buy a sandwich. I began to cross a side-road in order to reach the café and as I was halfway across a car turned into the road at great speed and without warning and was almost upon me before I saw it. I didn't have time to move and was sure I was going to be knocked down and badly hurt, if not killed. I stood there, helpless, but felt an arm come from behind me holding me around my neck and then yanked me with force back to the pavement behind me. It happened very quickly. I was shaken and stood there, rubbing my throat where the arm had been, convinced it must be bruised and sore, but it was fine. No one was near me and, strangely, no one seemed to have noticed anything. I realised that I had been saved from a serious accident by my Guardian Angel. I was very grateful.

Other angels oversee the evolution of a place, a landscape, a region, a country, a continent, a planet, a solar system, a galaxy – and so on. Some angels work with animals and plants, helping them in their growth and well-being, others work with human beings in specialist roles: a children's angel, for example, will help those people who work to heal sick children or they will help children in need directly.

Angels who work with humans, while normally unseen, are very close to us and can be called upon at any time for help, even for very practical matters like clearing a bad traffic jam or making an onerous job easier. They are also very good at making their presence known at times when we may need reassurance or comfort, by leaving small white feathers in our path to show us they are close.

When I worked as a lobbyist, a colleague of mine in Westminster was, like me, coming to a point of disillusion and frustration with the soulless world of politics. She had to attend a difficult business meeting one day and sat there feeling uncomfortable and rather sad, knowing she could not continue with that career for much longer. She gazed out of the fifth-floor window at the November night sky and was amazed to see a shower of white feathers floating down like snowflakes in front of her window. She realised that the angels were telling her they were with her and she was not alone and that all was well.

Some artists have the ability to see or sense the angel who guides your life and to paint them for you. It is wonderful to be able to see the image and colour, and to feel the energy of one who is so close to you. Please see the Resources section for more information about who to contact if you would like to see a picture of your own angel.

Archangels

Archangels are the most senior of the angels and they are very close to God. The most well-known are Michael, Gabriel and Raphael, but there are others who include Ariel, Metatron, Uriel and Haniel. Each archangel represents a particular quality – Raphael represents healing, for example, and Jophiel stands for beauty. You can call on any archangel to help you if you are in need of the assistance that they can give you specifically. Ask to be taken to them, by name, just as you are going to sleep or into meditation and see what happens.

The elements of nature

Every object on Earth has its own energy and in the world of nature each rock, plant, tree and animal has an aspect of Spirit associated with it, also a connection with one of the four elements of Air, Water, Fire and Earth, just as you do. The fifth element is Ether, or Spirit, which is in the core of everything. So, minerals and the soil, all that has substance, are connected to the Earth element. Whatever has emotions, flows or is watery is connected to the element of Water; what flies, communicates, or is to do with sound is the element of Air; while anything to do with energy is Fire.

A mighty Spirit of Earth, Air, Fire and Water presides over each respective element. They are very powerful and must be treated with great respect. It is possible to ask to get to know them and to work with them, but it is wise to do this only when you have a good understanding of the implications and what to do.

During the summer of 2007, a shamanic friend of mine became tired of carrying cans of water to his orchard for some young apple trees he had planted recently in Herefordshire. He decided to do some ceremonial work, calling in the Spirit of Water to bring rain. Unfortunately, he did not specify how much or when it should cease, and as a result contributed to a three-month period of torrential rain.

In the nature-spirit hierarchy, below the Spirits of the Elements are the Elementals. These are:

Earth	Air	Fire	Water
Gnomes	Sylphs	Salamanders	Undines
Elves		Fire giants	Mermaids
Brownies			Nymphs
Dryads			Water fairies
Goblins			
Trolls			
Fairies			

Between them they govern everything in their kingdom of Earth, Air, Fire and Water. They are hard to see, but you may sometimes spot a small ball of light in your fireplace which is a salamander, an unusual human-shaped cloud which is a sylph, a graceful female form swimming under a waterfall or riding a wave, or glimpse a flash of movement in a tree root or under a blade of grass, which is a gnome of some sort.

Elementals are happy to help you, indeed, they thrive on human attention and company. You may call upon them, preferably as you are walking in nature or in the element to which they belong, to help you in different ways if you have a problem:

Gnomes (Earth)	Money matters, stability, endurance, security
Sylphs (Air)	Inspiration, creativity, communications, intellect
Salamanders (Fire)	Power, courage, conflict, determination
Undines (Water)	Emotional issues, love, friendship, addiction, desire, sex

Never deceive or misuse an Elemental.

If you are interested in learning more about the elements of nature, you may wish to read William Bloom's book *Working with Angels, Fairies and Nature Spirits*.

Power Animals

Just as you have spirit guides who help you to learn a particular lesson for a period of time, like my harlequin who taught me about joy, so you have animal totems who accompany you, and only you, to help you as you are developing certain aspects of yourself and also to give you protection. Some are with you throughout a lifetime, some pass through just long enough to do their teaching job with you before retreating quietly to the shadows.

They may not have physical bodies, but power animals are very real and are a highly important part of your team of spiritual helpers. You may have one, two or more with you and they never leave your side.

I have three power animals: one is a big cat who walks in front of me, one is a bird who always sits on my left shoulder and the third is a mythical creature who walks on my right. The cat is for courage, the bird for wisdom and the mythical animal, who has only recently joined me, is for spiritual purity and strength. They have their own names and characters and are wonderful companions as well as assisting me practically in many ways. They help me if I am doing psychopomp work, as I discussed in Chapter Five on Light and Dark; if I am not well they will chase away the bugs from my body; they protect me from any negativity that may be around; and they take me where I need to go if I do any shamanic work, again protecting me along the way. If I work with a Spirit of the Elements, I ensure they are present and alert.

You may identify your power animals and how to work with them through learning some simple shamanic techniques and good classes are available. Shamanic 'journeying' using your power animals is a powerful and effective spiritual tool and I recommend it highly to those of you who are interested in working and connecting with the world of nature, in getting spiritual insight and information as well as getting to know your animal totems.

The Spirit of your home

Every place has its own spirit and this also applies to the place where you live. It is rather like a guide who cares for the well-being of a house or even a room, just as your guides look after you. Many people are unaware that their home has such an entity and even those who understand the concept can be unaware of the importance of being on good terms with it.

If you ignore or offend the Spirit of your place it can make life difficult for you. You may find that equipment breaks down, that there are leaks, or that you feel uncomfortable or unhappy there. The ways you can upset Him or Her (it may have a masculine or feminine energy) are by ignoring the Spirit or by treating your home without appreciation or honour – being very untidy, for example, or neglecting to maintain it.

The Spirit wishes to be acknowledged and appreciated and if you co-operate you will find your home runs smoothly and you will be content. This process of working together begins even before you have moved in. When a house or flat is for sale, its Spirit will assess every person who views and will, if necessary, create an energy or situation to ensure they do not proceed. It wants the right person to be there.

If you see a house and fall in love with it, I suggest you find a way to be alone in it, in the centre of the place if you can, in order to connect with the guardian and ask for its support and assistance to enable you to buy it. Assure it of your good intentions! It will assist the process enormously for you.

If you have decided to move house and you find that it does not sell for some mysterious reason, it may be because you have not told the Spirit of your intentions and involved it in your decision. It may sound unbelievable, but I have seen the proof of this for myself and other people.

The way to do it is to sit quietly and to ask for the Spirit of the Place to come to you. When you believe it is present, explain why you are planning to move and say that you will be leaving with love and gratitude for all the care, protection and happiness you have experienced there. Tell it that you will endeavour to attract the right people to replace you, ones who will also love the place and who will benefit from being there. Finally, ask it to release you from the place to enable you to move on freely.

Whenever I have been staying somewhere, whether it is a house for years or a hotel room for a night, I give thanks to it when I leave for its protection and gift of shelter. When I arrive for the first time, similarly I greet its spirit and ask it to care for me. It is a small ritual I perform meticulously on arrival and departure and I feel the benefit from doing so, always.

CONNECTING WITH *YOUR* HELPERS

Now that you have an idea of the many different categories of spiritual helpers there are, you are in a position, if you wish, to see if you can connect with the beings of light and love who are part of your own personal team. The more you can get to know them, to sense their different energies and characteristics, the better able you will be to work comfortably and knowledgeably together. Remember, you are the head of the team, spearheading your joint mission on Earth, and like every good team leader, the closer you are to your team members the more you will all achieve.

First of all, however, you may wish to get a sense of who is supporting you. A good way to get a sense of your non-physical team members is to do a meditation and I suggest you do it in the following way:

A meditation to identify and connect with your spiritual helpers

Before you start your meditation, remind yourself of the different categories of helpers there are – guides, Masters, animals, angels and so on, but without expectation of what may apply to you personally. Keep an open mind for now.

- Prepare for your meditation in the usual way, not forgetting to set your intention (which is to identify and connect with some of your helpers) and to put protection around yourself.

- Take three deep breaths.

- Mentally or vocally ask for one of your helpers to make itself known to you. Do not specify of what sort or source.

- Wait and see if an image, a sense, a fragrance or a sound

comes to you to indicate if it is, for example, an archangel, a relative, your Master or someone else altogether. The impression may be fleeting, but do not disregard it. When you are using your intuition, it is the first piece of information that comes to you that is most valid, but then, almost invariably, your chatterbox mind will come in to challenge that impression and tell you what is more logical – and it is usually negative. So it is in this situation too. Be alert to every message or sign that comes to you and do not dismiss it as fantasy.

- When you get a connection, you may wish to explore a little further to see if it is someone you have known or if they have a name. Identification may be vague or indistinct to begin with but you will find that more and more information comes to you as you do this exercise again and again, if you are willing, and you will be able to sense them and communicate with your helper increasingly easily over time.

- Having got to know who one of your helpers is, you can repeat the exercise to identify others who are working with you if you wish. Eventually you will get to the stage when you can ask them questions and request their assistance for what is going on in your life.

While this meditation is aimed more at helping you identify and get to know your helpers, another very powerful meditation is given at the end of this chapter which is intended specifically to help you connect and communicate with one or more of your own spiritual helpers. The daily meditation practice given at the beginning of this book will also be useful.

Here are some of the other ways of connecting and asking for help:

- Prayer is a very powerful way of connecting. I suggest it should not be ritualistic or formal and certainly not deferential – you are invoking the help of your equals, your team members.

- Write a letter or note to your helpers. The letter will be like writing to your best friend or the person you trust most in the world. You may start it with 'Dear Guides', for example, or 'Dear Helpers in Spirit'. If you have a name, then you can use it here also. You may then pour your heart out to them, saying how you feel, what you want, what the assistance is that you require. It is essential that you are totally honest both to yourself and also to them, and also very clear as to what it is you are asking for. If there is any ambiguity you may get an outcome you did not want.

  When you have written your letter – and it does not have to be lengthy – you will burn it afterwards, on a fire if you have one or with a match in a bowl or sink. As you do so, remember that you are consigning it and its contents to the world of Spirit, for action. Never ask for anything that is not for the highest good, or, if you like, is not ethical nor in the spirit of greatest integrity.

- Chat to your helpers mentally or vocally as you are doing household chores and about anything you like, however trivial or specific.

- Before an important meeting or event, such as if you are going to give a speech, ask your helpers to help you prepare for it and to support you through it. Explain what it is all about and what you want to achieve. At the time of the event, mentally gather them round you: you may well feel their warmth and love as they do so. They will understand why they are there and that they are there to help you throughout the experience. It really does make a huge difference to how you feel, and the outcome, if you remember to do this. Don't forget to thank them afterwards for their help and presence.

- Drum, dance, sing, chant to call them to you. Your helpers love music and beautiful creativity.

- First thing in the morning and last thing at night, think of them lovingly and thankfully and thank them for all they do for you.

WHAT CAN YOUR HELPERS DO?

Your assistants in spirit can help you in very many ways. I have talked about how they can help you through a daunting work event already.

Additionally, you can ask them to help you if you have got lost, if you or someone you love is ill, if some sort of physical disaster occurs, if the washing machine breaks down, if you are feeling miserable, if you want to see the sunshine.

Remember that your helpers are there to assist you in a very personal way, and so if you want to help the starving children in Africa you may wish to call on the help of God to bring peace to the world, in general terms, and use your own direct helpers to guide you as to what you can do yourself to help in those circumstances.

Because you don't know what karma is being played out in a particular situation, such as in Africa, it is important to refrain from judging what is going on and imposing on it what may be an incomplete or distorted understanding. This is why, instead of saying, 'Please stop the wars and corruption in XYZ places', places where the wars may be part of the learning for those peoples, it is wiser to ask for what you know is harmless and positive, like asking for love and peace everywhere.

You can ask for their help for anything in your life, but I suggest strongly that you do not request anything from your spiritual helpers that is not very well intentioned and for the highest good. It could result, at the very least, in negative karma, and would be unlikely to be successful.

As soon as you start to work consciously with your helpers, their ability to help you will grow and grow as your relationship with them does also. The cosmos is teeming with non-physical spiritual beings and many of them are waiting to help make your journey through life as productive and easy as possible if you are willing. They may be souls you know very well, perhaps as part of your soul or Ray group or souls you have known in past lives. Others are in a different category altogether but still focused on helping you.

It is important to understand what assistance from the world of Spirit is available to you and to use it wisely and with gratitude. It is the greatest wish for these ones to work with you and support you in your journey through life, to see you grow as a spiritual being, and by asking for their assistance your core aim as a soul, to evolve as rapidly as possible, will be facilitated. The more you can connect with them, the more successful this will be.

Exercise 8 : Meditation to connect with your spiritual helpers

- Prepare for meditation in the usual way.

- Take three deep breaths and focus on your breathing for a few minutes, until your mind is quiet and still. Don't worry if stray thoughts come and go, just draw your attention back to your breathing if this occurs.

- Gently say to yourself or out loud that it is your intention to connect with whichever of your spiritual helpers is appropriate for you at this time and ask them to join you. Think about what this means, for a moment.

- Turn your awareness to the energies around you and see if you feel a change in the energy, a presence, perhaps smell a fragrance or hear or feel something, even if it is just a breeze on your cheek. If you feel nothing, don't worry.

- Focus now on your heart. In your mind's eye see a two-pointed perfect multi-faceted diamond form in your heart and watch it grow bigger and bigger until it envelops you, one point behind you and one point in front.

- See the point of the diamond that is before you open up like a window. Walk towards it and you see a platform leading from the diamond window into the blackness of the universe. The platform itself is brightly lit.

- Leave the diamond and walk out onto the platform. Walk along it until you see in the far distance someone or something walking towards you. If you feel willing, continue walking until you meet your spiritual helper.

- Greet your helper and speak with him/her/it. You may wish to ask its name and purpose, and if there is work for you to do together. You could ask other helpers to join you there. It is up to you.

- When your conversation is over, ask your helper(s) if there is a gift for you. Receive it with thanks and love. Whatever it is, it will have a symbolic meaning for you.

- Thank your helper(s) and return to the diamond. Allow it to seal its window onto the universe and then to reduce in size until it is enclosed in your heart once again.

- In the knowledge that you can use your diamond vehicle to revisit your helpers at any time, gently close down your chakras, put protection around yourself and return to your everyday reality.

- Note down what you have experienced in your spiritual journal.

Chapter Eight
The Universal Laws

In this chapter I will be looking at some of the great Universal or Spiritual Laws, the ancient but perennial Truths which encompass every aspect of living as a spiritual being.[1] What I have given to you so far about what it means to be spiritual is underpinned by these Truths, which are based on principles of common sense and which apply to every era throughout history and to people of every age.

There are over 100 of these great Laws. They are so old their origins are lost in the mists of time, but spiritual teachers like Alice Bailey and Helena Blavatski revived knowledge of them in the nineteenth and early twentieth centuries, as a result of their own research and information that was channelled to them. Since then they have faded into obscurity again which is a pity in view of the important guidance they offer to help our path as humans and as souls and to help build that connection to Spirit.

More recently a number of books have been written purporting to be about the Spiritual Laws, but many of them are a loose interpretation of just a few of the Laws, focusing on aspects of self-help, personal development and so on. While in their own way they can be helpful, the true Laws are much more profound particularly when considered in their totality.

WHY THE LAWS ARE IMPORTANT

The Laws describe how to behave and be in order to maximise our spiritual potential, but they also explain much about our cosmic links and spiritual heritage. The purpose of this chapter is to consider the key Laws which apply to you and which are the foundation for the philosophy of this book. I encourage you to read them through, with my explanations, because, if understood and practised, they will expand your spiritual potential greatly. They will also maximise your enjoyment of your life journey and revolutionise your way of thinking and being.

Certain Laws may attract you over others and it is likely that the meaning and importance of these particular ones have a particular significance at this time in your life. I suggest that you look at them carefully to see why this is so. However, all of them are of great interest and when you look at them as a whole you will see the coherence and pattern they form. By understanding what they mean, however broadly, you will understand, literally, the meaning of life, of being spiritual and the meaning of God.

I believe this may be the first time that these Laws have been considered in modern-day terms in this way, which is remarkable given their importance. If everybody in the world lived according to the Laws, or with an understanding of them, then our human society would be coming from a very different place with peace, harmony and kindness prevailing over self-centredness and materialism.

In this chapter I will be looking at the ten Laws which relate particularly to the teachings in this book, with examples and advice to help you apply them to your own life. The other Laws are listed, with further explanation, in Appendix 1. If you have the time and the inclination, I would encourage you to read them through also, for together with what is put forward here they provide a vision and explanation for all that is, anywhere, particularly with reference to your own soul journey. They encapsulate spiritual wisdom.

THE TEN KEY LAWS FOR SPIRITUAL WISDOM

1. The Law of Attraction

This is one of the three major Laws and it is tremendously important. It governs the soul and is to do with like attracting like (like a magnet), and this may be in a positive or a negative sense. Sometimes you will attract what you want or need (or what you don't want) and sometimes you will drive away what you crave because of your fear of not having it. So, if you are desperate for money your fear of not having it will drive the opportunities for acquiring it away from you. If you are focused on poverty then this is what you will attract. If you focus in happy anticipation on your beautiful new home, then that is what you will draw to you. It is all about the power of thought, which we considered in Chapter One on being spiritual.

Everything about your life and in your life is governed by this Law. The people who are around you – friends, partner, spouse – your work, even your health are as they are as a result of this Law. So, if you are in an abusive relationship it is because you have attracted it to you: you want to punish or hurt yourself and so your energy, your vibration draws to you what you want, albeit subconsciously. If you have a broken leg, it may be that you brought an accident to you in order to rest, to get sympathy and attention, to avoid having to go to work, to delay doing something unwelcome. Have an objective look at your life, at who and what is in it. Where it is unsatisfactory, consider what in you has made it so, has attracted that dynamic to you.

Remember, everything that you attract is for your learning, in the most positive sense. As such, this Law underpins every chapter in this book.

2. The Law of Cause and Effect

This is very important for those on a spiritual path. It states that whatever we do has an effect and that nothing happens by chance. So, 'as you reap so shall you sow' applies very aptly here. It is closely related to the Law of Karma and applies to the karmic principles which are discussed in Chapter Two.

A good example of the working of this Law concerns a friend of mine who was house hunting and thought she had found her dream house. Problems to do with planning permission arose from unauthorised improvements done earlier and she pulled out at the last minute using this as an excuse, causing great inconvenience to many people. The real reason was that she had changed her mind. When she came to sell her next home having herself done some improvements without the necessary planning permissions, her house sale fell through in exactly the same circumstances as had occurred to her. It was like a boomerang coming back to hit her.

So, you see, if you do something that is perhaps a little unkind, thoughtless or malicious, something very similar will occur to you too. If you are able to observe your actions before you undertake them to ensure they are ethical and from the heart, with best intentions, you will know the outcome, whatever it is, will be the best one possible for everyone involved in that situation. A loving action will bring love to you, a negative action will not be so good.

3. The Law of Cycles

This Law explains how everything, anywhere, has its own cycle and time. So, the moon rises and sets at a particular point in a particular way, as does the sun. Women have a menstrual cycle, the seasons come and go. The Earth has cycles of being very cold and very warm, spirituality has its cycles also, sometimes being very prevalent or very distant. The great cycles of time and of Light and Dark, you may remember, were discussed in Chapter Five. Indeed, cycles have been a recurring and important theme throughout this book.

As an individual, you have times when you are busy or quiet, when you are at rest or in a time of change. You have cycles of learning and cycles of lives. It is very important to recognise the cycles in your life and around you and to 'go with the flow'. Don't try to interfere with your cyclic pattern, but allow everything to evolve in its own time and own way. Do not force change but accept whatever cycle you are in, in the knowledge that in its own time it will change. If you try to resist a cycle you will be resisting the energetic flow and it will become blocked.

4. The Law of Divine Flow

This is about living in the present and not brooding on the past nor fearing, anticipating, what lies ahead – much of which may never happen. We cannot change the past but we can change our attitude to it, accepting what we have done or experienced as, always, an opportunity to learn or grow – and then putting it behind us with gratitude for what it has taught us. My own experiences that I mentioned in Chapter One are a good example of the wisdom of this law.

It is hard to switch to being totally in the Now when you have been so used to being somewhere else in your mind. Practise. When you are, for example, composing a letter, stroking your cat, washing up, cleaning the bathroom sink, walking to work, focus as hard as you can on what you are sensing. Hear the noise your pen is making on the paper, feel the softness of the fur, be aware of the hot water, smell the Fairy Liquid, listen to your footsteps on the ground, notice the coldness of the basin. If you are able to get into the habit of concentrating on what you are doing every time you can, it will expand your consciousness and grow your spirituality tremendously.

5. The Law of Expansion

This relates to the universe and beyond and how it is constantly expanding. Similarly, the consciousness within you is expanding also at the rate you choose and you have no limit as to how far you can grow as a human and as a spiritual being – which are one and the same in actuality. The more you allow yourself to expand without inhibition or blocks, the more your energies flow freely and you can then attract anything you want or need to facilitate that growth into your life. So, the Law of Expansion works beautifully with the Law of Attraction.

The key to working with this Law is to ensure that you do not resist. When you are in resistance you will feel slowed down, sluggish, emotional and 'stuck', all of which are signs that your energetic connections, your spiritual links, are not flowing freely. When you are working with the Law of Expansion you will feel joyful, contented, abundant and confident. If some negativity creeps in, look to see what you are resisting, laugh with yourself and then do something about it. The energies will then begin to flow freely again.

This Law relates to the chapters on 'The Soul's Journey' (Chapter Four) and 'What Does It Mean to Be Spiritual?' (Chapter One) in particular.

6. The Law of Flexibility

This is all about self-awareness and acceptance, seeing that everything you do or that comes to you is for a purpose, recognising that a problem is actually an opportunity. It is about pragmatism and non-judgement and relates to Chapter One.

If you are able to understand the usefulness of this Law, you will see that it refers also to outcomes. If you are rigid or insistent upon a particular result then there can be no flexibility or spontaneity in what you do and Spirit is unable to guide you as much as it can. If you are open to your path and the outcomes in your life, having goals and visions certainly but without being insistent upon achieving them in a specific way, then you are not placing any limitations upon your potential and opportunities. This allows for unlimited expansion.

7. The Law of Meditation

If practised, meditation brings about, at the very least, a calm mind if regularly and appropriately undertaken and is an excellent tool to assist spiritual growth. There are many different systems of meditation, some are simple and quick, others are complex and lengthy; some involve music, prayers, chanting, some require special breathing techniques and postures, some need a teacher. In the end it is up to you to determine which form of meditation, if any, is appropriate for you and what you hope to get from it. Some people believe that meditation can bring enlightenment. Buddha found enlightenment after meditating under the Bodhi Tree.

Meditation must, as in all things, be undertaken with moderation and a sense of balance. If you spend many hours of the day in meditation on a regular basis, this can be self-indulgent, escapist and can leave you ungrounded – a bit spacey if you like. It is fine for monks, but for people who are living in the twenty-first century with occupations, families, everyday commitments and responsibilities, there usually is not the time anyway and it is not particularly desirable. I recommend half an hour a day as a maximum. For some people, five or ten minutes a day thinking creatively about their goals, visions or higher matters is sufficient. Guidance on a regular meditation practice is given in A Note about Meditation at the beginning of this book.

8. The Law of Non-Attachment

This says that, by overcoming your wish or need for money, possessions and stimulants, all of which are addictions, and by having no emotional attachments, you can achieve spiritual enlightenment. Then, nothing matters.

Attachment is one of the hardest habits to break and is one of the most significant impediments to your becoming spiritual. Have a look at your life and see what is the biggest attachment you have? What do you most fear losing or being without? Is it your home? Is it your money? Is it how you look? Is it what people think about you? Think about how bad your life would be without them. Would it really be that bad? What is the worst that could happen?

Remember, an attachment is all about your own need and fears, and an attachment to people in your life, whether it is your children, your partner or your friends can often be a reflection of your own insecurities. In this situation, if you are able to change the attachment to unconditional love for these important people in your life, you are taking the neediness away. Some people dread their children growing up and leaving home because of how it will affect them: that is attachment. Others wave them good-bye cheerfully and wish them well, genuinely, whatever they are feeling inside: that is unconditional love – doing the best for those that they love, and putting their interests first.

The chapters on 'What Does It Mean to Be Spiritual?' (Chapter One) and 'The Soul's Journey' (Chapter Four) are underpinned by this Law.

9. The Law of Patterns

This refers to old or obsolete patterns and those which are useful to you. Any pattern that you recognise as destructive or unhelpful you can break through awareness, intention and effort. You can reinforce useful patterns through focus, understanding and determination.

What is there in your life which just doesn't flow well? For example, do you find relationships are constantly ending up badly? Are you always in financial difficulty? Are people always arguing with you? Do you always have a weight problem? These are patterns, some of which you may have had over many lifetimes not just this one. Every pattern is a reminder of a belief or fear you have, such as that you are not worthy of being loved, that you fear being in a long-term relationship and so sabotage the possibility, the belief that you don't deserve to have money, or that having money is unspiritual. Many of these belief patterns are very old and when you see them for what they are, then you can make a conscious effort to change them. If your intention is clear, you will be successful.

The chapters on 'Karma' (Chapter Two), 'What Does It Mean to Be Spiritual?' (Chapter One) and 'Life, Death and Reincarnation' (Chapter Three) relate to this Law.

10. The Law of Unconditional Love, or the Law of Love

This is another key Law. It is about giving honour, respect and compassion within the umbrella of love to every living thing, including yourself. This is the heart of spirituality and the heart of this book. By honouring others, and yourself, in this way you are honouring their soul's journey also. You are using your higher self to connect with theirs and the love of the divine flows also through this interaction.

I am not talking here just about unconditional love between two people. You can give unconditional love to everything everywhere by opening your heart and sending out your great love to the whole planet and even beyond. Unconditional love means you do not want to get anything back in return, there is no quid pro quo in your mind or a desire for reward – but the wonderful thing about giving love unconditionally is that you get everything back you could want. Everything flows, life is easy and joyous and filled with abundance. A marriage based on unconditional love on both sides will always be strong.

Unconditional love is unselfish love, asking nothing from another or others but it is giving from the heart. However, because the gift of love is so great, it is impossible for you not to have anything in return, and the more you send out heart-felt love, the more it will return to you in abundance. Practise opening your heart every day and sending out your love to those you know and those you don't, to the world of nature, the world of spirit. If you are having difficulties with someone, send your love to them and it will help heal the situation. Don't have conditions, expectations or judgement for these are incompatible with unconditional love.

Exercise 9: Identify your key universal laws

- When you have read through this chapter on the Universal Laws, and glanced through Appendix 1 if you can, please close the book and sit for a moment with an empty mind.

- Ask yourself, 'Which Law or Laws stand out for me?' It is very probable that a phrase or word reflecting one of the Laws will come to you. If it is more, that is fine.

- Open the book again and reread the paragraphs relating to the Laws you have identified.

- Then please reflect upon what the words mean for you and your life now, and what their significance may be.

- Decide what you would like to do next to draw those particular Laws more strongly into your life.

- As always, please make notes in your spiritual journal to remind you of what you have learned and now intend to do.

Epilogue (The Future)

So, the book that so nearly was not written is complete and I thank you with all my heart for having kept me company through these pages. I feel myself so blessed to have been given the means, since my spiritual awakening, to remember and relearn the wonderful spiritual truths which make up this book. I am hugely grateful for the opportunity that has been given to me to distil my knowledge in this way and to pass it on to you. It has been a joy.

I am curious to know what you think of my book? While I have tried to make it as accessible and clear as possible, I know the topics we have considered together are complex in parts, that some of my ideas contradict accepted opinion, and that I have confronted head on certain subjects which are seldom talked about publicly, like death.

Whatever your views, I hope it has given you food for thought, at least, and a greater understanding of yourself as soul and spirit. Above all, I hope you have a sense, now, of the cosmic and divine totality of which you are a part, and the perfection and order of your spiritual lineage and connections. If my words have helped the light of one reader only to shine more brightly, my work will be done, my purpose achieved in my writing.

A GLIMPSE INTO THE FUTURE

Before we part company for now, I would like to share with you some of my thoughts about what lies ahead for us, pulling together the predictions I have given from time to time in the course of *Spiritual Wisdom* and adding to them as you will see.

The ascension of the planet

Just as you are reaching a certain point on your soul's journey, Earth is reaching a time when she will move to another higher dimension as part of her own soul's progress. She will become a sacred planet and as such her role in the solar system will be pivotal. She will be a planetary centre for cosmic communication and the men and women who are living with her will be a part of this great work. This is so important and exciting!

As part of this process, people are choosing, at the level of the soul, whether they wish to be included in the new world order that will follow the ascension of Earth. Whatever they choose to do, whether to be a part of it or not, there is nothing right or wrong in their decision. Those who choose *not* to be a part of it will continue their lives and soul journey much as before, but they will be living on a planet that looks like Earth does now, but which will, in fact, be a distance away. Their new planetary home may be part of the Pleiades. It will feel in every respect like a third-dimensional world of materialism and the men and women who have chosen to be there will continue learning their lessons as before. When they are ready, there will be the opportunity to rejoin their peers on Earth.

Those people who have chosen differently will move with our planet to her new dimensional home and will assist the work of creating planetary and inter-planetary connectedness. This does not mean, necessarily, they will die! Just as we move into different dimensions as we progress on our soul's journey and go through different initiations of learning, often still in the same body, so it will happen to the planet and those who go with her. Our light will shine brighter; otherwise we will be the same.

Additionally, humanity will, once again as we were long ago, be a loving bridge between the world of nature and the world of spirit.

Earth will be a different place altogether from what it is now. Communities large and small will live and work together in peace and co-operation in an ethos where kindness and thoughtfulness prevail, where leadership comes from integrity and wisdom, and where all the kingdoms of nature, including man, are in balance, honoured and appreciated for what they are and what they give. This is the new Golden Age to come.

Earth changes

Because of the imminence of her spiritual expansion, the planet is beginning to stretch and flex her muscles, like a sleeping giant awakening. She is getting ready to be reborn, just as many men and women among humanity are feeling their own birth pains as they prepare to move to another level also. This is causing some physical repercussions, such as extremes of weather, volcanic activity and earthquakes. These will continue for the next few years. Water, in particular, may be excessive, even overwhelming.

I believe there are further dramatic changes to come, including physical upheaval and a rebalancing of resources. In certain parts of the world, where there was little water, for example, there will be plenty, where there was lush vegetation there will be desert. The seas and rivers may flow differently and the Earth plates may shift, changing the appearance of the landscape. Whole continents may move. It is possible that, because of overload and Earth changes, the electrical grid system in many countries could be threatened and the Internet, as a means of communication and connection, could crash altogether, bringing about disruption to the financial centres in particular.

These changes are not to be feared. They are not Armageddon or the end of the world or the end of life on Earth. They are to do with the spiritual expansion of the planet. Humanity will be part of this wonderful and auspicious process and what is to come after it.

Meanwhile, at the moment, a polarisation of opinion is taking place between those who see, increasingly, what is occurring physically and who wish to take measures to ease the birth pains through energy conservation, sustainable farming and local community co-operation, and those on the other hand who either deny there is a problem or put commercial priorities above the pressing need to change the way we live. This is such a pity and such a wasted opportunity. It is another Earth lesson being learned, but not very well!

New technologies

Nothing can stop the ascension of planet Earth, but there is time to make the transition as comfortable as possible, for everybody, despite the politicians! Excellent and imaginative ideas are beginning to come forward, but the pity is that, so far, the politicians who could make them happen, our 'leaders', seem not to have the will or the courage to do so.

As I write, in 2008, scientists, researchers and innovators are developing new technologies that will enable our energy needs to be provided economically and without harming the environment. Some people are talking of encouraging and enabling every home and building in their home country to be self-sufficient through wind and solar power.

I believe that more and different ways to utilise the energy of the sun will be discovered. It will be used not only for heat and light, but also as part of new ways of communicating. The Internet as we know it now will be replaced by sophisticated systems using the sun in conjunction with as-yet undiscovered minerals, crystals and other materials.

Despite or perhaps because of the impotence of world leaders, people in many parts of the world are starting to anticipate the likely further Earth changes. There is a resurgence of interest in growing vegetables, developing local co-operatives, coming 'off the grid', and some large corporate companies are putting their governments to shame by their determination to do what is morally right for the environment, not what would seem to be in their commercial best interest. They have the wisdom to see that by working in co-operation with the planet they will benefit everybody.

Time and space

Already time is changing. You may have noticed an acceleration in time for yourself and felt as if everything is topsy-turvy. You may have found yourself forgetting simple things like appointments, birthdays, names and have wondered if you were getting memory problems. You are not: you are anticipating the change in time that approaches.

I believe time as we know it will cease and one day we will live in the present only, with no thought of the past or the future. It will be a little scary at first, but there will be great benefits when you get accustomed! Imagine instantaneous travel, no queuing at airports or travel delays . . . you will learn to create a thought, an intention, a wish and through the power of your thought it will manifest itself. This is how it used to be and how it can be again.

For you personally, because you are likely to be living and working in a higher dimensional sphere, you will find the vibrations around you are much more refined because there will be less dense physical matter. One of the reasons why so many people are finding being alive quite uncomfortable at this time is because their vibrational level is having to rebalance itself with that of the planet, which is changing rapidly.

When you have 'recalibrated' yourself you will be even more attuned to the spiritual spheres: your psychic skills will be more developed and you may find you are able to communicate telepathically one day. Indeed, eventually words may become almost obsolete as spiritual sensitivity and attunement, soul to soul, predominate on Earth once again.

CONCLUSION

The coming new Golden Age is not a dream. It is not even a 'prob-able'. For me it is a certainty and the more that people like you and I aspire to expand our spiritual horizons, to do our best, the sooner it will come. Through our understanding and awareness, our intentions and actions we really can change our lives and our world. Let's do it, together.

I would love to receive your thoughts and views on what I have taught in Spiritual Wisdom. If you would like to contact me, please do so via my website, www.inluminoglobal.com, or by writing to me care of Piatkus Books. While I will try to answer every genuine message, I cannot guarantee that I will be able to do so personally.

Appendix 1
Further Universal Laws

1. The Law of Abundance

This is the ability to manifest abundance in all things, not just money, but friendship, peace and so on. The Law states that there is no limit on the abundance that is available to you and that the only limitation is that which you impose yourself through your lack of belief or inability to set the intention clearly.

You must have care in using this Law, because you can invoke an abundance of negatives also, such as poverty or suffering. Abundance means quantity and so by asking, 'Please bring abundance into my life' you could be asking for an abundance of unhappiness, of misfortune and so on. Ask for positive abundance instead or be specific in asking for an abundance of joy.

2. The Law of Action

This concerns bringing our potential to life through our actions and being able to manifest our visions, aspirations and intentions.

3. The Law of Analogy, or Correspondence

This teaches us that we are the microcosm of the macrocosm,

and that everything that exists has its corresponding principle beyond it. 'As above, so below.'

How you are internally is reflected in your surroundings and your surroundings reflect your inner world similarly. So, if you are feeling confused, upset, demotivated, beset by doubt, fear or anger, you may find your home is untidy, cluttered, possibly even a little unclean with dirty dishes in the sink and your sheets needing changing. Or, it could be sterile, pristine but cold and uninviting if you really don't like yourself. Your neighbourhood, by extension, could be noisy, unruly with difficult neighbours. Have a look at your surroundings and see how far they reflect what is going on inside you. See what could be changed. It is amazing how decluttering, spring cleaning, putting flowers in the house can change how you feel about yourself.

4. The Law of Akasha

This is one of the greatest of the cosmic Laws and it governs the existence of everything that is, has been or will be in the future. It is the Law of Eternity, and it orders the existence of events, matter, consciousness and the other Laws. It also allows the keeping of the Akashic Records, which are the records of everything and everyone at any time in the past, present or future. This Law cannot be used or abused by humans, it is inviolable, and any attempt to use it or the Records for personal gain will backfire.

5. The Law of Ascension

This Law defines the vibrational frequency of a soul and how the level strengthens and raises as the soul gets closer and closer to merging with its divine source, until the process of ascension at the seventh Initiation takes place. This is discussed in detail in Chapter Four.

6. The Law of Balance

This is the Law dealing with fair exchange and is all about having balance in every aspect of your life. Earth is a planet of balance and part of your learning is to bring balance on to the Earth itself through your actions and also into your own life, so that everything is operating harmoniously as a whole and in its individual components.

It is important to have balance in the small things in life as well as the big. When you are eating, do you do so even if you are not hungry? Do you eat everything on your plate whether you are full or not? If you are in a place of balance you will eat when your body tells you it is time and just enough to satisfy you without being excessive.

If you are in a discussion with someone, how often do you resist the opposite views, until the situation becomes argumentative? Under the Law of Balance it is important to honour your views and those of others, and to accept the right of others to express how they feel openly and freely as they should honour yours.

How balanced are *you*?

7. The Law of Challenge

As you become more spiritually aware you may become sensitive to the presence of non-physical beings. These are discussed in Chapter Seven. If you wish to communicate with them and are not sure if the answers you are getting are accurate, or are from your imagination, then by asking your question three times you will get an accurate response.

If you become aware of a presence around you and it makes you uncomfortable, you can say three times, 'In the name of God, if you are not of the highest good then go', and the energy will leave.

8. The Law of Chemical Affinity

This is to do with the preservation of the mineral kingdom and the coming together of atoms.

9. The Law of Cohesion

This Law is very complex and, at higher levels, is to do with the divine spark within you. At a more prosaic level it concerns the way atoms and particles are drawn together to seem to 'cohere', so that the chair you are sitting on seems solid, for example.

10. The Law of Colour

This Law deals with the effect of colour upon your body, mind and emotions. When certain colours are directed at specific parts of the body, they will bring about change which can be profound when used in specific ways.

Colour therapy can be very powerful, but you do not need a therapist, necessarily, to use it. You can do a lot yourself. For example, if you paint your walls pink, wear pink clothes, put pink flowers in your home, you are encouraging love to you, you will feel more gentle and loving and your heart will open.

11. The Law of Common Ground

This applies when you have a difference with someone. By coming together and talking about it, reaching a compromise, the misunderstanding can be resolved. This is all part of the Law of Balance. Mediation occurs under this Law.

12. The Law of Compensation

This is a sub-law of the Law of Cause and Effect and reminds you that you will get back what you put in. So, if you have good intentions and try your best you will get back the abundance you deserve.

13. The Law of Consciousness

This Law relates to the expansion of consciousness. As your consciousness expands through your increasing spirituality, so the opportunities for growth and abundance expand to become limitless.

14. The Law of Continuity of Consciousness

This is about the merging of your individual consciousness with the universal consciousness, which results in your total spiritual knowing, your merging with the divine which is your spiritual goal. Self-awareness is a critical step towards achieving this total knowing and union.

15. The Law of Cyclic Return

This Law concerns the wheel of rebirth, whereby under spiritual contract you agree to complete a complete cycle of life on Earth (see Chapter Three) over many lifetimes in order to achieve a certain level of spiritual awareness.

16. The Law of Discipline

This is all about clarity and commitment to our intentions and our goals. Unless we have discipline and understanding as to what we want and where we wish to go, if there is confusion or uncertainty, vacillation or procrastination, we will not get what we want nor where we want to be.

Focus, as part of the Law of Discipline, is very important. Please think about a recent goal you have created for yourself. Consider how far it was successful or where it fell down. What discipline did you put into it? How clear and focused were you?

17. The Law of Disintegration

This relates to the final absorption of the soul into the divine within you at the sixth initiation, which is discussed in Chapter Four. It refers to the disintegration of the final vestiges of that which has held you in the world of matter, the third dimension.

18. The Law of Divine Love and Oneness

This concerns our interconnectedness with everything and how eventually we reach the point of being totally connected with Spirit and are a spiritual Master.

19. The Law of Economy of Force

This Law governs life on Earth and is to do with the best use of time and energy. It is the third of the three major Laws. It is actually all about common sense and doing everything calmly and expeditiously without undue effort.

20. The Law of Expectation

This Law says that by changing your expectations you can change what happens to you. This is, again, all about the power of thought and intention. If you expect to be poor, then you will be. If you expect your relationships always to be disastrous, then the chances are they will be.

In fact, having expectations at all is not necessarily helpful because it is focusing on a hope or fear which is rather different from having an intention. There is a big difference between expecting to be mugged and intending to be mugged – one is passive and has some uncertainty (you may expect an inheritance but it is not assured), the other is active (I intend to do my best at work today). So, instead of having expectation you may wish to create a clear intention instead. With expectation can come disappointment.

21. The Law of Faith

This Law is about having belief in yourself. There is so much wisdom and knowledge within you, far more than you believe because you, through your interconnectedness with all, have access to all the universal truths. Your chatterbox mind may deny this, remind you that you did not do well at school and draw comparisons with academics, people on television, even your colleagues. However, you have a lot of intuitive knowing within you and if you allow your intuition – which is the link with the universal wisdoms – to guide you in your life it will help you in your decision-making as well as your spiritual growth.

For one hour or one day or one week, allow yourself to be guided totally by your intuition. If you are shopping, buy what you feel instinctively is good for you to have, not what your mind tells you. If you are driving and have the urge to turn down a side street then do so, for there will be a reason to go there. If you feel like taking a day off work to go to the sea, then do so if you can. Any decision you have to make, go within and ask yourself, 'What is the appropriate action for me now?' You will be amazed by the results. Your intuition is your best friend, you know, and links you to all your helpers in the world of Spirit.

22. The Law of Fixation

This relates to your conception in any lifetime, and how the time of conception is one factor that establishes the blueprint for your life and all your lives.

23. The Law of Forgiveness

This Law is about love – accepting others with gentleness and understanding, with no wish for retaliation. Forgiveness must come from the heart. Words of forgiveness mean nothing if the genuine wish and intention to forgive is not there.

Sometimes you know that you 'ought' to forgive someone but it feels uncomfortable when you try to do so. If you are in a relationship, for example, and your partner goes off with your best friend, it is likely to take some time to come to terms with the situation and your resulting hurt and anger, however understanding and spiritual you are. Do not try to force yourself to forgive them, but allow the emotions you feel to come through. There is likely to come a time when you can see these events more clearly and in context, perhaps see how you contributed to the situation. That is the time when you can forgive, including forgiving yourself, and the forgiveness will feel good and will be meant. It will also be effective.

24. The Law of Free Will or Choice

Earth is a planet of free will and as such creates huge opportunities for people to evolve spiritually. Every human experience is made through choice and is a learning opportunity, so whatever you do, whatever decisions you make, however trivial, impacts upon your spiritual growth.

If you choose to spend many lifetimes learning about what it means to be poor, that is fine, but eventually, one day or one lifetime, you will choose to move on to another lesson when you have learnt enough. So, if you have issues to do with money, remember that through setting your intentions and being self-aware you can choose to move away from poverty whenever you are ready.

25. The Law of Gender

This Law decrees that all life forms contain the masculine and feminine, and this Law concerns sexual reproduction. In spiritual terms, the Law deals with the Divine Masculine and the Divine Feminine, which are the two key aspects of God. Eventually humanity will come to see that the masculine and feminine are one, and you will see yourself as a fusion of masculinity and femininity in perfect balance.

26. The Law of Good Will

This is about your role with the world at large. It concerns your attitude to world events, how you react to them, and how far you see yourself as being part of the world or even national community.

It is helpful to see what is happening in international affairs with detachment, understanding and compassion. Many people get emotionally caught up when they hear about a world disaster, child abuse, cruelty to animals and they do not see that, by so doing, they are hurting themselves by the negativity of their grief, anger or sadness, and that they are blocking any chance of helping the situation. By seeing the bigger picture, seeing that there is a reason for these events, by refusing to get caught up in the emotion, you can then send loving thoughts non-judgementally to the situation and the victims, and indeed to the perpetrators. This is a constructive use of the Law of Good Will, or Will Power.

27. The Law of Grace

Under the Law of Grace, if you are focused on your spiritual work, on healing, on trying to do your best in some respect or other, then the purity of your intention can waive something that would otherwise have been karmic.

If you are driving, but praying for the recovery of someone whom you know is very ill and, because you are so focused on the prayer you inadvertently drive through a red light, it is likely that, under the Law of Grace, the camera would be broken, no one would be hurt and you would not be reported.

28. The Law of Group Life

This Law encourages you to think beyond yourself, to see yourself as part of a group, a community and to do what you can to help that community. It is the antithesis of selfishness.

29. The Law of Group Progress

This refers to the fact that, when you see yourself as part of a group or community, you will find that the shared group effort will help you overcome all obstacles. 'A problem shared is a problem halved.' It serves also to remind you that as you are evolving as a spiritual person, you are not doing it on your own.

30. The Law of Healing

This Law is about precisely that – how by intention, focus and technique you can send or give healing to another using your hands or other forms of your energy. Healing is connecting with the divine energies and transmitting it to the object of healing.

31. The Law of Higher Will

This is about surrendering the lower nature of your personality –

fears, emotions, attachments and so on – in order to allow your spiritual self to come through.

32. The Law of Honesty

This Law is about honesty and self-awareness about yourself, and seeing others and everything clearly but non-judgementally without wishing to change it for your own benefit or desire. It is about truth.

33. The Law of Intention

This Law is about how energy follows thought, word and deed. I have talked a lot in Chapter One about the importance of intention in moving to a more peaceful, balanced way of living and being. Being aware of your intention and of the power your intention has to impact on your life and world is one of the most important changes you can make to become more spiritual.

34. The Law of Intuition

This teaches you that as you claim your spiritual identity so increasingly your intuitive faculties will strengthen. If you depend on or choose the opinions or knowledge of others over your own inner knowing it will inhibit if not prevent your intuition from operating to its potential. You will be controlled by factors outside yourself, which is a form of disempowerment.

There are a number of different ways by which you can access and identify your intuition. If you have to make a choice or decision and wish to practise using your intuition, then do this: focus on your heart. Take one of the choices you have – whether to go on holiday to India or China, say – hold it clearly in your mind so you are thinking of India and then put the image of you on holiday in India into your heart. You will feel something, a warmth, perhaps, or a weight. Do the same in thinking about going to China and see how that feels in your heart. One choice will feel different from the other, one will feel light and good, the other heavier, more neutral. You then know which choice is right for you.

35. The Law of Inverse Proportion

This is about longevity. It is about breathing and teaches us that the slower our rate of breathing, so the longer we will live. It is said that the God Kings who walked on Earth thousands of years ago were able to live for aeons by using techniques such as this.

In order for the breathing technique to be fully effective it is necessary to learn to channel the breath through the chakras and the meridian lines in the body – the subtle centres. The meridian lines are energetic pathways related to the nervous system in the body.

If you practise slowing down your breathing rate, so that you are breathing as slowly as possible without it being painful, it will help your concentration, quieten your mind and assist you to reach a meditative state.

36. The Law of Justice

This Law concerns balance and relates closely to the Law of Karma. If you do a wrong to someone, for example, you in your turn will be wronged to redress the balance. It may not happen at once and the justice may be meted out by someone else, but it will happen. Sometimes justice takes a lifetime to be achieved, or indeed it can happen over a number of life-times.

37. The Law of Karma

This is examined in detail in Chapter Two but, briefly, it is another name for the Law of Cause and Effect. Karma is the record of everything you have ever thought or done, from your first incarnation to the moment you are reading these words. Whatever you do or think has an impact on your life and what happens to you.

38. The Law of Knowledge

This is about the application and use of knowledge and its energetic make-up. It is also about power, because the more knowledge you have about someone else, or a particular situation, the more you can use that knowledge to control or disempower. Blackmail is a good example of this.

Do not believe everything that is told to you. A lot of information that is given out in the media or from people you know comes from half truths, gossip or is inaccurate. Put your belief in knowledge that is first hand – what you yourself know to be true, what you have witnessed for yourself, or what you believe from your inner knowing. If you wish to learn from someone else, then ensure you use the wisest and most trustworthy teacher or informant. This is practising the Law of Knowledge wisely.

39. The Law of Magnetic Control

This teaches that every thought creates an effect which returns directly to you. If the thought is loving, you will receive love back. If your thought is unkind, that is what you will experience for yourself, even if it is from another source.

40. The Law of Magnetic Impulse

This Law concerns harmonious relations between two people or a group of people. It is known as the Law of Marriage, because it is all about union between two entities brought together by magnetic attraction.

41. The Law of Manifestation

This is, again, all about the power of thought. If you have a pure thought, clearly defined, and it is held and strongly energised, then that thought will become reality.

42. The Law of Miracles

This teaches that a spiritually evolved individual can, through will, belief and intention bring into manifestation anything he or she wishes.

43. The Law of No-Judgements

This reinforces the point I made in the first chapter that judgement is a human device to compare yourself to others favourably or unfavourably, to assess yourself or another against arbitrary standards set by society. The universe, God, does not judge. If you are judgemental, you will be judged back in equal measure by others.

44. The Law of Non-Intervention

This states that it is a spiritual offence to interfere in the karma or evolutionary destiny of another. You must allow people to make their own choices and decisions, as far as it is possible and appropriate, for this is part of their learning and growth.

45. The Law of One

This Law is all about God, and reminds you that everything is part of God and that God is in everything.

46. The Law of Patience

This is a reminder that all that is has its time and season and you must not try to hasten it. 'Patience is a Virtue.'

47. The Law of Perfection

This teaches you that every single thing that happens to you or that you do is for the greatest good, is perfect for your spiritual and physical journey. This does not mean it is enjoyable at the time, but you should in hindsight be able to see the value of all occur-rences and what they have taught you. As you evolve and your spiritual awareness grows, so this understanding becomes clearer.

48. The Law of Periodicity

This is about rhythm – the ebb and flow of seasons, cycles, life and the universe. Everything vibrates to a certain rhythm and it is important to recognise these cycles and to see them as part of the rhythm of God, to accept them, to respect them and to go along with them. This Law is sometimes known as the 'Law of Rhythm'.

49. The Law of Planetary Affinity

This concerns itself with the planets, their alignment and connections and their interactions. It is an obscure Law based on ancient science and is connected to the Law of Attraction.

50. The Law of Polarity

This could also be called the Law of Opposites. Everything has an opposite and if we find ourselves with a negative thought or emotion we can change it by focusing on the opposite to it.

If you find yourself in an argument with your partner and you are feeling exasperated, remember one time when he or she did something loving and wonderful for you and this will deflate the tension beautifully.

51. The Law of Prayer

Prayer is the precursor to meditation because through prayer you are asking to connect and communicate with your spiritual helpers in order that they can communicate with you during the meditation which follows. Prayer is also stand-alone, and the power of prayer to heal others and to bring about certain desired results can be very strong – if the intention is clear and the belief in the effectiveness of the prayer is there. Prayer should only be used for the highest good and with the best of intentions.

When you pray for a particular outcome, such as for the well-being of a loved one, always give thanks at the time and afterwards for what will come or has come as a result of your prayers. It brings the healing into the present, as opposed to it being an aspiration only, which is very important.

52. The Law of Process

This is all about identifying what needs to be done to achieve your goal and ensuring you follow your plan without skimping any of the steps to reaching that goal. Missing a stage can result in failure. It is also important, under this Law, to recognise and appreciate the value of each of the steps towards your goal as you are taking it.

53. The Law of Radiation

This Law refers to the ability of any atom, any thing, any part of you, to move from one sphere of energy into a greater expansion of consciousness and a higher vibratory level. So, once again it is all about expansion of consciousness and the importance of not letting anything block or limit your spiritual growth.

54. The Law of Rebirth

This concerns reincarnation and the reasons why we reincarnate from lifetime to lifetime. It is discussed in detail in Chapter Three. A true understanding and respect for this Law will encourage you to look carefully with detached awareness at what you do in any lifetime – your words, thoughts and actions are the key influences for your spiritual growth, and how far you evolve in this lifetime is the determinant for what is needed for your next incarnation.

55. The Law of Rebound

This gives you the ability to experience a difficult or painful situation and come out of it much stronger. Again, it is your choice to be weakened or depleted by it or to be strengthened. Choosing to rebound positively can result in a strong spiritual 'spurt' and often these situations are created in order to give this opportunity.

56. The Law of Rhythm

This is connected with the Law of Cycles, only this time it is focused on the balanced nature of the rhythms of our emotions, or the tides, for example. So, if you have strong mood swings, they will change from one extreme of intensity to the opposite, in equal measure. It is about movement (for nothing stands still), equilibrium, balance, and it is up to you as to which swing of the pendulum you choose – up or down, happy or sad, rich or poor, spiritual or not, just as nature chooses the rhythm of the seasons in any period.

57. The Law of Right Human Relations

This is about your behaviour and interaction with other people and the importance of tolerance, understanding and kindness, with no attempt to control or coerce.

58. The Law of Sacrifice (and Death)

This Law concerns the inevitable destruction of your body at a certain fixed time in order for your soul to move on in its evolutionary cycle, creating another body at some point afterwards – and again, and again, until the need to be reborn ceases.

59. The Law of Schools (or Love and Light)

This applies to you when you have reached a certain level of spiritual awareness and concerns the different levels of consciousness you will experience on your soul's journey.

60. The Law of Service

This Law is all about living, being and working in the world with an awareness for the needs of others, a wish to do your best and without attachment to getting personal gain or benefit from it. It summarises what I have written in Chapter One.

61. The Law of Sex

This is about the merging physically of male and female in the human kingdom. At times before in the history of man, when a very high level of spiritual consciousness prevailed, men and women were not biologically separate but rather were androgynous, and it is likely this situation of Oneness will return again when man has evolved sufficiently. Sex will not be necessary for procreation or as an expression of love between humans.

62. The Law of Solar Union
This is a very obscure consideration of the different aspects of divinity at work helping our planet, the solar system and the universe beyond, at many different levels.

63. The Law of Sound
This Law considers the powerful nature of sound and what it can do to heal and change you. Everything has its own sound even if you cannot hear it and you yourself have your own sound too. Music, chanting, prayer, affirmations aloud can raise your vibrational levels and bring about profound healing by changing and restoring harmonic patterns. The use of sound by groups, such as intoning or saying mantras, can produce amazing results.

64. The Law of Spiritual Approach
Again, this deals with subjects considered in Chapter One, this time about how your words, thoughts, deeds and actions create your reality and how 'good behaviour' will increase your spirituality.

65. The Law of Spiritual Awakening
This discusses the responsibility that comes with becoming spiritual. Being spiritual involves (without you necessarily knowing or thinking about it) being an example to others, and so self-awareness and some discipline in conduct and behaviour are necessary.

66. The Law of Summons
This Law is about soul connecting with soul to communicate or

express a message. At a certain stage in your spiritual evolution you will be able to do this without the need to be physically present together with the corresponding soul. This coming together of two souls often occurs when you are asleep and you may have dreams of the other individual and being with them which are strong and vivid. It may be someone in incarnation or in the non-physical.

67. The Law of Surrender

This is all about trust and it is one of the hardest Laws to adhere to on the spiritual path because it requires you to give up your old patterns of belief, your outdated habits, the familiar 'security blanket' of, for example, your boring but safe job or boring but safe marriage, and to surrender instead to the guidance of your intuition. It is about surrendering to the unknown, taking risks, doing something – often radical – when you do not know how it will turn out. Complying with this Law is one of the quickest ways to evolving spiritually.

68. The Law of Synchronicity

This says that there is no such thing as coincidence. Everything happens for a reason and at the perfect time and if, for example, you have been thinking of someone and a few moments later they call you, then it is because your thoughts have created the event. Sometimes it is more than the power of human thought and intention, but the power of the divine to manifest on Earth what is necessary for the balance and spiritual destiny of you yourself and the world.

69. The Law of Synthesis

This is the last of the three major Laws and is possibly the most important. While the Law of Attraction governs the soul and the Law of Economy governs the world of matter, the human world, this one governs the spirit and is about the interconnectedness and oneness of all. It is all about God and concerns your ability to transcend everything for total unity with the divine.

70. The Law of Teaching

This emphasises the importance of and need for people to pass on their wisdom to those who can benefit by it, for the sake of the continuity of the human race.

71. The Law of Telepathy

This concerns the ability of an individual to transmit thoughts to the mind of another person using the third eye chakra between the eyebrows, and for them to receive the thoughts in their heart centre. This ability has been dormant in most of mankind for thousands of years, but the ability to communicate telepathically is one which is available to you and which you might find yourself using as you raise your level of consciousness on your spiritual path.

72. The Law of Thought

In Chapter One I spent some time explaining about the power of your thoughts and how energy follows thought to create an outcome or reality. This is the Law which underpins the theory.

73. The Law of Three Requests

This is another aspect of the Law of Challenge, discussed above. It states that, by repeating a prayer or invocation three times it strengthens the energy behind it and the likelihood of the outcome you are praying for.

74. The Law of Time

This concerns the fact that the only time that exists is the present. It is in the Now that you create through your intentions, thoughts, words and actions, and it is in the Now that you live. You cannot live in the past, which is done and is a memory, nor the future which is created from what you are doing in the present. So, this Law is about living in the present, not living for what is done or in fear of what might happen in the future – both of which usually are emotion and fear driven. If you are able to live in the present you will see and sense what is actually happening around you and to you and appreciate it for what it is with clear vision and understanding.

Please see also the Law of Divine Flow, which also deals with living in the Now.

75. The Law of Unity

This Law reminds you, again, that you are connected with everything, even though when you are in human body you may have forgotten your divine source.

76. The Law of Vibration

This explains that everything in the universe is in motion. It moves and vibrates, and depending upon whether it is a manifestation of matter, a sound, a thought or something subtler will determine at what rate it vibrates. As you become more spiritual your vibrational rate will increase.

77. The Law of Will Power

This teaches that you can choose how far, when and in what way you can achieve your spiritual potential, and that your development is not dependent on the progress of others. It is quite a complicated law and relates to other lifetime experiences you have had or will have and what is happening to other souls who share your spiritual path.

References

Chapter One

1. There will be frequent references to Masters in this book. A Master is someone who has mastered all there is to know and learn about being human and living in the third dimensional world of matter. They may work in the physical or non-physical realms.
2. *Om Mani Pedme Hum* means 'Hail the jewel in the lotus' and is a prayer to achieve the compassion, purity and wisdom of the Buddha.

Chapter Three

1. A near death experience occurs after a life-threatening experience such as a bad car crash or after major surgery. You have come close to death or even seem to be clinically dead, but have then returned to life. Some people watch themselves from outside their bodies, see a tunnel of light ahead of them, and hear voices which may be telling them to go back because it is not time to leave their earthly existence. It is said to be a very peaceful and wonderful experience.
2. The etheric body is the energetic counterpart of the physical body and is like an electro-magnetic field. It is the energy, the vitality, which keeps the body alive. It is invisible, the same shape as your body and surrounds your body as part of your aura. Your chakras are housed within your etheric body.

3. Because the astral plane is so like the world they have left, many new arrivals believe that time as they knew it before still exists and act accordingly. In fact, there is no calendar or clock time. Eventually they may learn that they can manifest whatever they want instantly through their intentions and thoughts without having to wait for it or travel to it.

Chapter Four

1. Everything in physical manifestation vibrates at a certain frequency, including you as a human being. The higher or faster your vibrational rate, the more easily you can access the higher spiritual realms, even if you cannot see them. The lower your vibrational rate, the more you are associated with denser objects in the world of matter that you can experience physically. It is rather like a whistle: some pitches you can hear, others that are higher pitched can only be heard by animals and not the human ear. By learning to be more spiritual, you will raise your vibrational levels perhaps considerably.

2. Dimensions are divisions of the universe. The higher the dimensional level, the closer it is to God. Dimensions are also known as spiritual planes and the terms often are used together. So, the third dimension is the Earth plane in all its physicality, while the ninth dimension is the plane of the divine. As your consciousness expands and you become more spiritual, so you are able to work more and more in the higher dimensions, even while you are living on Earth.

3. The information given here is based principally on Alice Bailey's material in *A Treatise on Cosmic Fire*, *The Rays and the Initiations* and *Initiation, Human and Solar* (see Bibliography).

Chapter Five

1. One of these is Richard C. Duncan who wrote, controversially, *The Peak of World Oil Production and the Road to the Olduvai Gorge*.

2. John Major Jenkins among others has written extensively on

the subject of the Mayan calendar and its meaning and 2012. His books include *Galactic Alignment and Maya Cosmogenesis*. If you are interested in this subject, I recommend Daniel Pinchbeck's *2012 The Year of the Mayan Prophecy*.

3. The Church teaches that Lucifer is the good angel, the Morning Star, who turned from God and fell from heaven, never to be forgiven.

4. An ancient order of Celtic Pagan priests who revere the moon, sun, stars and certain other elements of nature.

5. Followers of witchcraft.

6. In very exceptional circumstances you may witness a ghostly 'embedded memory' event in which you were involved at the time, but it is most unusual.

Chapter Six

1. Alice Bailey has written definitively and extensively on the Rays and those who have followed her on this subject, such as Joshua Stone, Zachary F. Lansdowne and Michael D. Robbins (see Bibliography) have, almost invariably, based their work on her teachings. The information that I give here is based on the works of Alice Bailey, in particular *Esoteric Psychology Volumes I and II* and *The Rays and the Initiations Volume V* and Michael D. Robbins' *Tapestry of the Gods*.

2. Taken from *Tapestry of the Gods Volume I*, pages 31–38 by Michael D. Robbins PhD.

3. Taken from *Tapestry of the Gods Volume I*, pages 45–56 by Michael D. Robbins PhD.

4. Taken from *Tapestry of the Gods Volume I*, pages 63–78 by Michael D. Robbins PhD.

5. Taken from *Tapestry of the Gods Volume I*, pages 89–108 by Michael D. Robbins PhD.

6. Taken from *Tapestry of the Gods Volume I*, pages 123–137 by Michael D. Robbins PhD.

7. Taken from *Tapestry of the Gods Volume I*, pages 145–155 by Michael D. Robbins PhD.

8. Taken from *Tapestry of the Gods Volume I,* pages 167–82 by Michael D. Robbins PhD.

9. This chart, compiled by me, summarises extensive information given by Michael D. Robbins in *Tapestry of the Gods Volume I.* I have adapted some of the wording and analysis to accommodate the purpose of this chapter without, hopefully, detracting from his meaning. He has made it clear that some of his ideas in this section are speculative based on his own research and beliefs. I have no reason to disagree with anything he has put forward.

Chapter Eight

1. The channelled works of Alice Bailey are the starting point for my understanding of the Laws and I have expanded on her guidance quite considerably in describing what they are and how they apply to us today. There are one or two brief summaries on the Internet which may be useful if you wish to explore the Laws further.

Bibliography

Books by Alice Bailey, published by the Lucis Press.
The Alice Bailey books listed here are those which have been helpful to me in writing *Spiritual Wisdom*. The list is not comprehensive. Please contact the Lucis Trust directly for further information and on how to obtain these and others of their publications.

Initiation, Human and Solar (published 1922)
Letters on Occult Meditation (published 1922)
A Treatise on Cosmic Fire (published 1925)
A Treatise on White Magic (published 1934)
The Destiny of the Nations (published 1949)
Discipleship in the New Age Vols I and II (published 1944/1955)
The Reappearance of the Christ (published 1948)
Telepathy and the Etheric Vehicle (published 1950)
The Externalization of the Hierarchy (published 1957)
A Treatise on the Seven Rays:
    Vol I – Esoteric Psychology (published 1936)
    Vol II – Esoteric Psychology (published 1942)
    Vol V – Rays and Initiations (published 1960)
Bloom, W., *Working with Angels, Fairies & Nature Spirits*, Piatkus, 2002
Campbell, J., *The Power of Myth*, Bantam Doubleday, 1989
Cooper, D., *A Little Light on Ascension*, Findhorn Press, 1997
Cooper. D., *A Little Light on the Spiritual Laws*, Findhorn Press, 2007

Goldstein, J. and Kornfield, J., *Seeking the Heart of Wisdom,* Shambhala Publications, 2001

Graf, S., *The Cosmic Game,* State University of New York Press, 1998

Jones, A., *Opening your Heart,* Piatkus, 2007

Lansdowne, Z.F., *The Rays and Esoteric Astrology,* Motilal Banarsidass, 2002

Pinchbeck, D., *2012: The Year of the Mayan Prophecy,* Piatkus, 2008

Robbins, M.D. PhD, *Tapestry of the Gods Volumes I and II,* Univ of the 7 Rays, 1988

Samanta-Laughton, Dr M., *Punk Science,* O Books, 2006

Stone, J.P. PhD., *The Complete Ascension Manual,* Light Technology, 1994

Zukav, G., *The Seat of the Soul,* Rider & Co, 1991

Resources

UK

Spiritual Teacher, Lecturer, and Channel for Melchizedek
Inlumino Global (Claire Montanaro)
01597 811 110
mail@inluminoglobal.com
www.inluminoglobal.com

Past Life Regression
Janet Thompson
mailme@janetthompson.org

The Transformation Game and Past Life Regression
Yvonne Hill
yvonnehill@btinternet.com

Astrology – gateway to the soul
John Fallick
jwfallick@aol.com

Personal Development and Mentoring
Lee Teresa Lott
01547 560 046
lee@leeteresalott.com
www.leeteresalott.com

Spiritual Healer and seminar speaker
Anne Jones (includes release of karmic vows)
01425 403 228
anne@make-ripples.org
www.annejones.org

Shamanism – classes, soul retrievals and healing
1. The Sacred Trust
01258 840 392
mail@sacredtrust.org

2. James Weaver
07759 983 767
jgweaver@btintenet.com

Reiki Masters (training and healing)
1. Julia Shepherd
07890 644 753
julia@juliashepherd.com
www.juliashepherd.com

2. Jane McPherson
jane@soulsoother.co.uk
www.soulsoother.co.uk

3. Claire Montanaro
(training only)
Contact details as above.

Geopsychic and geopathic healing (includes release of negative entities)
Debbie Rye
01638 742 022

Angel Paintings
Everyday Angels (Alison Knox)
0115 985 6878
everydayangels@btinternet.com

Essences and Sprays
International Flower Essence Repertoire (www.healingflowers.com)
Hazel Raven (www.hazelraven.com)
Aura Soma (aura-soma.net)

Colour Therapy
Aura Soma (www.aura-soma.net)

Environmental and Ethical Organisations
Friends of the Earth (www.foe.co.uk)
Greenpeace (www.greenpeace.org)
British Trust for Ornithology (www.bto.org)
Buglife (www.buglife.org.uk)
Froglife (www.froglife.org)
Bat Conservation Trust (www.bats.org.uk)
The Woodland Trust (www.woodland-trust.org.uk)

The Lucis Trust

For information on the Alice Bailey and other publications, and its educational work to promote spiritual values and activities in the world.

Suite 54

34 Whitehall Court

London SW1A 2EF

020 7839 4512

www.lucistrust.org

Aristia

An independent, principled, supplier of crystals, books and spiritual artifacts

01983 721 060

www.aristia.co.uk

AUSTRALIA

Spiritual Teacher, Lecturer, and Channel for John the Beloved (Helen Barton)

johnthebeloved@bigpond.com

Clinical Gestalt Psychotherapist, Teacher and Guide (Sharon Snir)

+61 2 9924 2192

Sharonthru12@optusnet.com.au

CYPRUS

Healing, Teaching and Channelling (Anna of Cyprus)

+357 269 30388

info@onetouch-centre.com

www.onetouch-centre.com

NORWAY

Homeopathy, Acupuncture and Theta Healing Body Alignment
(Bjorg Jeppesen)
+47 22 140 664
b.jeppesen@combitel.no

USA

Seven Ray Institute (Michael D. Robbins)
For Ray Pattern Profiles
+1 201 798 7777
sevenray@sevenray.com

MAGAZINES

Caduceus (cutting edge articles on spirituality)
Kindred Spirit (a very popular new Age Magazine in the UK)
Pagan Dawn (pagan, Wiccan and folklore issues)
Permaculture ('solutions for sustainable living')
Resurgence (ecological and spiritual analysis and discussion)

Index